Preliminary Edition Notice

You have been selected to receive a copy of this book in the form of a preliminary edition. A preliminary edition is used in a classroom setting to test the overall value of a book's content and its effectiveness in a practical course prior to its formal publication on the national market.

As you use this text in your course, please share any and all feedback regarding the volume with your professor. Your comments on this text will allow the author to further develop the content of the book, so we can ensure it will be a useful and informative classroom tool for students in universities across the nation and around the globe. If you find the material is challenging to understand, or could be expanded to improve the usefulness of the text, it is important for us to know. If you have any suggestions for improving the material contained in the book or the way it is presented, we encourage you to share your thoughts.

Please note, preliminary editions are similar to review copies, which publishers distribute to select readers prior to publication in order to test a book's audience and elicit early feedback; therefore, you may find inconsistencies in formatting or design, or small textual errors within this volume. Design elements and the written text will undergo changes before this book goes to print and is distributed on the national market.

This text is not available in wide release on the market, as it is actively being prepared for formal publication. This may mean that new content is still being added to the author's manuscript, or that the content appears in a draft format.

If you would like to provide notes directly to the publisher, you may contact us by e-mailing studentreviews@cognella.com. Please include the book's title, author, and 7-digit SKU reference number (found below the barcode on the back cover of the book) in the body of your message.

THE
READING-WRITING
THINKING CONNECTION

YOUR THOUGHTS YOUR VOICE

PRELIMINARY SECOND EDITION

Suzanne Borman, William Borman,
Sylvia Garcia-Navarrete, Joel Levine,
and Yuki Yamamoto

cognella®

SAN DIEGO

Bassim Hamadeh, CEO and Publisher
Seidy Cruz, Specialist Acquisitions Editor
Carrie Montoya, Manager, Revisions and Author Care
Kaela Martin, Project Editor
Casey Hands, Associate Production Editor
Emely Villavicencio, Senior Graphic Designer
Alexa Lucido, Licensing Manager
Natalie Piccotti, Director of Marketing
Kassie Graves, Vice President of Editorial
Jamie Giganti, Director of Academic Publishing

Cover image: Copyright © 2014 iStockphoto LP/simonkr.
Copyright © 2016 iStockphoto LP/Jacob Ammentorp Lund.

Printed in the United States of America.

3970 Sorrento Valley Blvd., Ste. 500, San Diego, CA 92121

To Dr. John D. McNeil for his lifelong commitment and selfless service to the well-being of others through education.

To our families and dear friends, whose love and support made this work possible.

CONTENTS

PART I   EDUCATION AND SOCIAL ISSUES   1

SECTION 1
Reading-Writing **Thinking**

SECTION 2
Writing-Reading **Thinking**

PART III   SCIENCE AND PSYCHOLOGY   335

SECTION 1
Reading-Writing **Thinking**

INTRODUCTION

Each word of the title of this book, ***The Reading-Writing, Thinking Connection:*** *Your Thoughts Your Voice*, has been chosen to communicate to you a clear sense of what you will experience as you progress from class to class through the semester.

Perhaps the most important words in this title are Your Thoughts Your Voice. **To this point you have experienced joys and sorrows, and struggles and successes in education, as well as what you have seen in life. Your thoughts, feelings, and ideas—**Your Voice**—need to be heard and given expression as a contribution to the common good of those around you and for your own well-being.**

The understanding and skill you gain through the "thinking-centered" approach to education used in this book will give you the solid foundation needed to progress through your further journey in higher education and life. With continued use of OUR THINKING TOOLBOX you will gain confidence both in your ability to communicate your thoughts in writing and to understand and speak about what you read in the areas of education, social issues, history, philosophy, science, and psychology.

OUR THINKING TOOLBOX consists of 16 specially designed Tools. Each Tool engages your mind in a specific way. There is a large and complex cumulative effect when several of these Tools are used together as you read and as you write. A "culture of thinking" will be created in the classroom as you and your teacher use these 16 Tools. Most importantly, you further realize that the quality of your reading, writing, and learning are directly related to the quality of your thinking. By using OUR THINKING TOOLBOX under your teacher's caring and thoughtful guidance, you will holistically and systematically acquire both the standard mechanics-oriented reading comprehension skills (e.g., main ideas, supporting details, inferences, vocabulary) and writing skills (e.g., thesis statement, topic sentence, body paragraph, rhetorical analysis), as well as the focused thoughtfulness and understanding that is created in a thinking-centered classroom.

You will see that each of the 16 Tools has an "R" version and a slightly reworded "W" version. The "R" version of each Tool will help you understand what someone had to say so you can form your own thoughts about what has been communicated. The "W" version will help you to communicate clearly what you have to say so others can understand exactly what you want to express. Thus you will come to see through direct experience that reading and writing are two sides of the same coin.

Further, the "Strategies for Teaching and Learning" that your teacher will use with you provide the instructional practices through which the thinking-centered Tools will most effectively spark your initiative and curiosity, as well as stimulate your thinking as you progress from activity to activity and class to class. In this classroom environment, the Tools and Strategies used will guide you and give strength to your voice about critically important topics.

30 CLASS MEETINGS: COURSE DESIGN AND FOCUS

Six Discipline Areas

The 30 class meetings you will experience as you use this book are organized into 3 parts around 6 discipline areas: *education, social issues, history, philosophy, science, and psychology.* The ideas and information you gain in these areas will be essential to your continued journey through higher education. As you use the "16 thinking-centered Tools," which comprise OUR THINKING TOOLBOX to read and write about topics in these discipline areas, the thoughts you create will open up a world of understanding.

PART I: **Education and Social Issues** (classes 1–4 focus on Reading, classes 5–14 focus on **Writing**)

PART II: **History and Philosophy** (classes 15–17 focus on Reading, classes 18–27 focus on **Writing**)

PART III: **Science and Psychology** (classes 28–30 focus on Reading)

Class Design

Each class meeting has a specific **Focus** with an *Opening Activity (OA)*, a *Main Activity (MA)*, a *Closing Activity (CA)*, and *Homework (HW).*

Our Thinking Toolbox

You will use the 16 Tools of OUR THINKING TOOLBOX through all 30 classes. The "R" version of these Tools will be used in the classes focused on Reading, and the "W" version in the classes focused on **Writing**. (Note: See pages 379–380 in the appendices for the complete set of Tools in OUR THINKING TOOLBOX).

Strategies for Teaching and Learning

The **Strategies for Teaching and Learning** used in each class meeting will help you think clearly in a focused way and gain confidence in your ideas so that your voice can be heard. (Note: See pages 381–394 in the **appendices** for all **12** Strategies for Teaching and Learning.)

PART I

EDUCATION
AND
SOCIAL ISSUES

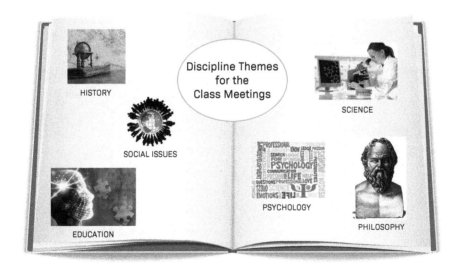

HISTORY

SOCIAL ISSUES

EDUCATION

Discipline Themes
for the
Class Meetings

SCIENCE

PSYCHOLOGY

PHILOSOPHY

<u>Focus</u>: Analysis of Speech by César Chávez and Opinion Paper

OA   Quote, John Dewey

MA   Speech, César Chávez

CA   Discussion, Topic Ideas

HW   Opinion Paper

"What is worth learning is worth learning well."

—Alfred North Whitehead

Opening Activity

Directions

- Turn to a partner.
- Identify who is person A and who is person B.
- Complete the sentences that follow.

A

My first main RESPONSIBILITY as a reader is to ...

_____

_____

_____

_____

B

My first main RESPONSIBILITY as a writer is to ...

_____

_____

_____

_____

My first main responsibility as a reader is to **understand** what someone is trying to communicate to me in writing.

My first main responsibility as a writer is to **communicate clearly** so that others understand what I have to say.

You will use 16 tools from OUR THINKING TOOLBOX in this course. The two **support tools** that follow provide guidance on how to better <u>understand</u> what you read and more <u>clearly communicate</u> what you have to say as you write. (**R** version helps you when you <u>read</u> and **W** version helps you when you <u>write</u>.)

SUPPORT TOOLS

D O X I TOOL	**R**	For a word (concept) in the reading that you think you need to understand better: look up the **D**efinition; put it into your **O**wn words (i.e., paraphrase it); give an e**X**ample of it; **I**llustrate it.
	W	For a word (concept) you want to use in your writing that you think you need to understand better: look up the **D**efinition; put it into our **O**wn words (i.e., paraphrase it); give an e**X**ample of it; **I**llustrate it.
GRAMMAR TOOL	**R**	Notice how the author selects and arranges words in his or her sentences to express what he or she wants to say (i.e., parts of speech, tenses, punctuation).
	W	Select and arrange words in your sentences to express clearly what you want to say (i.e., parts of speech, tenses, punctuation).

Directions

- Turn to a partner and identify who is person A and who is person B.

- Read the quote that follows.

- Paraphrase the quote. In other words, capture exactly what Dewey (person "A") or Locke (person "B") communicates to us *in your own words*.

A

"The aim of education should be to teach us how to think, rather than what to think."

—John Dewey

_____

_____

_____

B

"Reading furnishes the mind only with materials of knowledge; it is thinking that makes what we read ours."

—John Locke

_____

_____

_____

Main Activity

Directions

- Read the speech by César Chávez that appears on the following pages.
- Respond to the **prompts** that follow using the "<u>R</u>" version of each tool provided.
- Respond in clear and complete sentences (thoughts)—except #3.

1. What do you think was the "specific" **TOPIC** César Chávez focused on in his speech?

_____

_____

_____

TOPIC TOOL	<u>R</u> Identify the specific topic that the author has written about.

2. What do you think was the main **PROBLEM** César Chávez raised in his speech? Explain why you say this.

_____

_____

_____

PROBLEM TOOL	<u>R</u> Identify the main problem or issue focused on in the reading that needs to be addressed. Explain why this is a problem.

3. I think César Chávez's most important **CONCLUSION** about education in California was ...

_____

_____

_____

CONCLUSION TOOL	<u>R</u> Identify what you think is the most important conclusion that the author came to in the reading and how that conclusion was reached.

4. Copy the **INFORMATION** that made you think this was the most important conclusion César Chávez came to in his speech. (Note: Place quotation marks around the sentence(s) you copy.)

_____

_____

_____

INFORMATION/ REVIEW OF LITERATURE TOOL	<u>R</u> Identify information and ideas that support and illustrate important points made by the author in the reading.

5. Create a **TITLE** for this speech by César Chávez.

TITLE TOOL	<u>R</u> Create a title that expresses the main idea (focus) of the reading.

Title:

Some people may ask, "Why should the farm workers be concerned about the condition of public schools in California?"

Let me answer them: Who do you think are in the public schools today in California?

Public schools serve more farm workers than any other publicly financed social institution in society.

Public schools provide the greatest opportunity for upward mobility to Hispanics and to all ethnic minorities in this state.

Yet today, it is a Republican governor and his allies in the legislature who are less concerned than we are about preserving public schools. That is ironic because it was not always the case.

In the 1960s and early '70s, another Republican governor—Ronald Reagan—was leading the fight for more support of public education. But there was a big difference. Back then, the majority of public school children were white, and they were from middle- or upper middle-income families.

Today, the majority of children in our public schools are minority—African American, Hispanic, Asian—and they are from poor and working-class families.

Back then, under Ronald Reagan, Californians spent 5 cents out of every dollar of personal income on public schools. Today, under Pete Wilson, Californians spend a little over 3 cents out of every dollar on education. And if he has his way, it will go down even more.

There is another institution in society that is funded by the state and that is dominated by minorities: the state prisons—and they have fared very well.

Over the last nine years, under Governor Deukmejian and now Governor Wilson, California has carried out a policy of dramatically expanding state prisons while it starves public schools.

What message do those priorities send? Does this mean that the only way our sons and daughters can get recognition from the state of California is by using drugs and committing crimes?

We have looked into the future and the future is ours! Asians and Hispanics and African Americans are the future in California. That trend cannot be stopped. It is inevitable.

Then why do they want to cut funds for schools and other vital services—now?

Why do Governor Wilson and his allies seek to reduce the commitment to public education—now? If the majority of children in school were white and if they lived in affluent suburban communities, we wouldn't even be debating how much money to spend on public education.

But it is *our* children—the children of farm workers and Hispanics and other minorities—who are seeking a better life. It is for them, for their future—and for the future of California—that we must say "no" to suspending Proposition 98.

We must say "no" to cutting essential services for the needy instead of tax loopholes for the wealthy.

We must say "no" to making *our* children and *their* teachers' scapegoats for the budget crisis.

Source: Cesar Chavez, "Statement from Cesar Chavez, Sacramento, April 3, 1991," *The Words of Cesar Chávez*, ed. R. Jensen and J. Hammerback, pp. 150-151. Copyright © 2002 by Cesar E. Chavez Foundation. Reprinted with permission.

Figure 1.1: Source: Copyright © Joel Levine (CC by 3.0) at http://commons.wikimedia.org/wiki/File:Cesar_chavez_crop.jpg.

Closing Activity

Directions

- Add two of your own ideas to the list of problems that follow that César Chávez spoke about in his speech.

- Underfunding of Public Education
- Growth of Prisons
- Racism of Government Leaders
- _____
- _____

We are now going to prepare to write an opinion paper about a problem César Chávez raised in his speech that particularly caught your attention.

Directions

- Respond to the prompts that follow using the "W" version of each tool provided.
- Respond in clear and complete sentences (thoughts)—except #5.

1. What **PROBLEM** from César Chávez's speech will you focus on in your paper? Explain why this problem particularly caught your attention.

PROBLEM: _____

WHY: _____

_____

PROBLEM TOOL	W Identify the main problem or issue that is the focus of your writing. Explain why this is a problem.

2. After reading César Chávez's speech, what is your **POINT OF VIEW** on the problem you have chosen to write about?

_____

_____

_____

POINT OF VIEW TOOL	W State your point of view (opinion) on the main problem raised in your writing.

3. Select a **quote** from César Chávez's speech to support your point of view.

_____

_____

Tell how this quote supports your point of view.

_____

_____

SPEAK IN THE AUTHOR'S VOICE TOOL	**W** Include quotes (or paraphrases of quotes) from selected authors or sources to support and clarify what you want to express in your writing. Cite relevant sources accordingly.

4. **PARAPHRASE** the quote you selected for #3. In other words, capture exactly what César Chávez said using your own words.

_____

_____

_____

PARAPHRASE TOOL	**W** Paraphrase a sentence(s) from what you read to use in your writing.

5. Create a "working" **TITLE** for your opinion paper.

_____

TITLE TOOL	**W** Create a title that expresses the main idea (focus) of your writing.

Homework

Directions

- Write an opinion paper about the problem César Chavez raised in his speech that particularly caught your attention.

- You responded to several **prompts** today. Use these thoughts to guide you as you write.

*Note: Include the **quote** you cited for the **speak in the author's voice** tool.*

GRAMMAR TOOL	**W** Select and arrange words in your sentences to express clearly what you want to say (i.e., parts of speech, tenses, punctuation).

Name: _____

Date: _____

Analysis of Malcolm X Autobiography Excerpt and Reflection on Video Discussion

OA   Quote, Virginia Wolf

MA   Autobiography Excerpt, Malcolm X

CA   Autobiography Excerpt, Malcolm X (continue)

HW   Reflection, *School to Prison Pipeline* (video)

"What is worth learning is worth learning well."

—Alfred North Whitehead

Opening Activity

Directions

- Read the quote that follows.
- **PARAPHRASE** this quote from Virginia Woolf's essay *A Room of One's Own*. In other words, capture exactly what Virginia Wolf communicates to us in your own words.

Figure 2.1: Source: http://www.loc.gov/pictures/item/94506886/.

"Lock up your libraries if you like; but there is no gate, no lock, no bolt that you can set upon the freedom of my mind."

—Virginia Woolf

_____

_____

_____

Main Activity and Closing Activity

Directions

- Read the excerpt from Malcolm X's autobiography on the following pages.

- Respond to the **prompts** that follow using clear, complete sentences.

1. What do you think Malcolm X's **PURPOSE** was for writing this excerpt?

_____

_____

_____

_____

PURPOSE TOOL	R Explain what you think the author wanted to accomplish through this reading.

2. Underline in the text what you think is the most **SIGNIFICANT SENTENCE** in this excerpt. Next, tell **why** you selected this as the most significant sentence.

_____

_____

_____

_____

SIGNIFICANT SENTENCE(S) TOOL	R Select the sentence(s) you think is the most important in the reading and tell why you selected it.

3. Ask Malcolm X a **QUESTION** about this excerpt to which you would really like to have an answer.

_____

_____

QUESTION TOOL	<u>R</u> Pose a thought-provoking question(s) to the author about something that caught your attention in the reading.

4. Use the **SPEAKING IN THE AUTHOR'S VOICE** Tool, and respond to the question posed above as though you were Malcolm X.

_____

_____

_____

SPEAK IN THE AUTHOR'S VOICE TOOL	<u>R</u> Express ideas, or answer questions, about the reading as if you were the author or an individual in the reading.

5. From this excerpt, what do you think Malcolm X **CONCLUDED** about the importance of reading in his life.

_____

_____

_____

_____

CONCLUSION TOOL	<u>R</u> Identify what you think is the most important conclusion that the author came to in the reading and how that conclusion was reached.

By Malcolm X

It was because of my letters that I happened to stumble upon starting to acquire some kind of a homemade education.

I became increasingly frustrated at not being able to express what I wanted to convey in letters that I wrote, especially those to Mr. Elijah Muhammad. In the street, I had been the most articulate hustler out there. I had commanded attention when I said something. But now, trying to write simple English, I not only wasn't articulate, I wasn't even functional. How would I sound writing in slang, the way I would *say* it, something such as, "Look, daddy, let me pull your coat about a cat, Elijah Muhammad—"

Many who today hear me somewhere in person, or on television, or those who read something I've said, will think I went to school far beyond the eighth grade. This impression is due entirely to my prison studies.

It had really begun back in the Charlestown Prison, when Bimbi first made me feel envy of his stock of knowledge. Bimbi had always taken charge of any conversations he was in, and I had tried to emulate him. But every book I picked up had few sentences which didn't contain anywhere from one to nearly all of the words that might as well have been in Chinese. When I just skipped those words, of course, I really ended up with little idea of what the book said. So I had come to the Norfolk Prison Colony still going through only book-reading motions. Pretty soon, I would have quit even these motions, unless I had received the motivation that I did.

I saw that the best thing I could do was get hold of a dictionary—to study, to learn some words. I was lucky enough to reason also that I should try to improve my penmanship. It was sad. I couldn't even write in a straight line. It was both ideas together that moved me to request a dictionary along with some tablets and pencils from the Norfolk Prison Colony school.

I spent two days just riffling uncertainly through the dictionary's pages. I'd never realized so many words existed! I didn't know *which* words I needed to learn. Finally, just to start some kind of action, I began copying.

In my slow, painstaking, ragged handwriting, I copied into my tablet everything printed on that first page, down to the punctuation marks.

I believe it took me a day. Then, aloud, I read back, to myself, everything I'd written on the tablet. Over and over, aloud, to myself, I read my own handwriting.

I woke up the next morning, thinking about those words—immensely proud to realize that not only had I written so much at one time, but I'd written words that I never knew were in the world. Moreover, with a little effort, I also could remember what many of these words meant. I reviewed the words whose meanings I didn't remember. Funny thing, from the dictionary first page right now, that "aardvark" springs to my mind. The dictionary had a picture of it, a long-tailed, long-eared, burrowing African mammal, which lives off termites caught by sticking out its tongue as an anteater does for ants.

I was so fascinated that I went on—I copied the dictionary's next page. And the same experience came when I studied that. With every succeeding page, I also learned of people and places and events from history. Actually the dictionary is like a miniature encyclopedia. Finally the dictionary's A section had filled a whole tablet—and I went on into the B's. That was the way I started copying what eventually became the entire dictionary. It went a lot faster after so much practice helped me to pick up handwriting speed. Between what I wrote in my tablet, and writing letters, during the rest of my time in prison I would guess I wrote a million words.

I suppose it was inevitable that as my word-base broadened, I could for the first time pick up a book and read and now begin to understand what the book was saying. Anyone who has read a great deal can imagine the new world that opened. Let me tell you something: from then until I left that prison, in every free moment I had, if I was not reading in the library, I was reading on my bunk. You couldn't have gotten me out of books with a wedge. Between Mr. Muhammad's teachings, my correspondence, my visitors—usually Ella and Reginald—and my reading of books, months passed without my even thinking about being imprisoned. In fact, up to then, I never had been so truly free in my life.

The Norfolk Prison Colony's library was in the school building. A variety of classes was taught there by instructors who came from such places as Harvard and Boston universities. The weekly debates between inmate teams were also held in the school building. You would be astonished to know how worked up convict debaters and audiences would get over subjects like "Should Babies Be Fed Milk?"

Available on the prison library's shelves were books on just about every general subject. Much of the big private collection that Parkhurst had willed to the prison was still in crates and boxes in the back of the library—thousands of old books. Some of them looked ancient: covers faded; old-time parchment-looking binding. Parkhurst, I've mentioned, seemed to have been principally interested in history and religion. He had the money and the special

interest to have a lot of books that you wouldn't have in general circulation. Any college library would have been lucky to get that collection.

As you can imagine, especially in a prison where there was heavy emphasis on rehabilitation, an inmate was smiled upon if he demonstrated an unusually intense interest in books. There was a sizable number of well-read inmates, especially the popular debaters.

Some were said by many to be practically walking encyclopedias.

They were almost celebrities. No university would ask any student to devour literature as I did when this new world opened to me, of being able to read and *understand*.

I read more in my room than in the library itself. An inmate who was known to read a lot could check out more than the permitted maximum number of books. I preferred reading in the total isolation of my own room.

When I had progressed to really serious reading, every night at about ten P.M. I would be outraged with the "lights out." It always seemed to catch me right in the middle of something engrossing.

Fortunately, right outside my door was a corridor light that cast a glow into my room. The glow was enough to read by, once my eyes adjusted to it. So when "lights out" came, I would sit on the floor where I could continue reading in that glow.

At one-hour intervals the night guards paced past every room. Each time I heard the approaching footsteps, I jumped into bed and feigned sleep. And as soon as the guard passed, I got back out of bed onto the floor area of that light-glow, where I would read for another fifty-eight minutes—until the guard approached again. That went on until three or four every morning. Three or four hours of sleep a night was enough for me. Often in the years in the streets I had slept less than that.

Source: Malcolm X and Alex Haley, "Learning to Read," *The Autobiography of Malcom X: As Told to Alex Haley*, pp. 174-177. Copyright © 1987 by Random House LLC. Reprinted with permission.

Figure 2.2: Source: http://commons.wikimedia.org/wiki/File:Malcolm_X_NYWTS_2a_cropped.jpg.

Homewerk

Directions

- In the link that follows, watch the video of *School to Prison Pipeline* from Democracy Now (https://www.youtube.com/watch?v=bEhv571cbX4).

- Respond to the following **prompts** in clear, complete sentences.

1. What struck you as the most important **PROBLEM** about what was discussed in this video?

_____

_____

_____

2. What is one particular part of this **PROBLEM** that you would like to further investigate? Explain **why**.

_____

_____

_____

_____

3. How would you begin to carry out this investigation?

_____

_____

_____

_____

Summary of Book Excerpt by Booker T. Washington and Strategies for Teaching and Learning

OA   Quote, César Chávez

MA   Book Excerpt, Booker T. Washington

CA   Strategies for Teaching and Learning

HW   Einstein Dialogue

"What is worth learning is worth learning well."

—Alfred North Whitehead

Opening Activity

Directions

- Read the quote that follows.
- **PARAPHRASE** this quote by César Chávez. In other words, capture exactly what *César Chávez* communicates to us in your own words.

"Students must have initiative; they should not be mere imitators. They must learn to think and act for themselves—and be free."

—César Chávez

_____

_____

_____

Main Activity

Directions

- Read the excerpt from Booker T. Washington that appears on the following page.
- Respond to the **prompts** in clear, complete sentences.

1. What do you think Booker T. Washington's **PURPOSE** was for writing these paragraphs?

_____

_____

_____

PURPOSE TOOL	<u>R</u> Explain what you think the author wanted to accomplish through this reading.

2. What **CONCLUSION** do you think Booker T. Washington came to about how to teach?

_____

_____

_____

CONCLUSION TOOL	<u>R</u> Identify what you think is the most important conclusion that the author came to in the reading and how that conclusion was reached.

3. What **INFORMATION** in this reading made you think this was the most important conclusion Booker T. Washington reached.

_____

_____

_____

INFORMATION/ REVIEW OF LITERATURE TOOL	**R** Identify information and ideas that support and illustrate important points made by the author in the reading.

4. What **QUESTION** would you like to ask Booker T. Washington about his ideas in this reading?

_____

_____

_____

QUESTION TOOL	**R** Pose a thought-provoking question(s) to the author about something that caught your attention in the reading.

5. Write a brief paragraph that captures the essence of what Booker T. Washington wants us to understand in this excerpt. To do this, use your responses to Prompts #2, 3, and 4, and any other **INFORMATION** in the reading.

_____

_____

_____

_____

_____

_____

_____

_____

6. Create a **TITLE** for this reading and write it in the box on the line that follows.

TITLE TOOL	R Create a title that expresses the main idea (focus) of the reading.

Title:

By Booker T. Washington

The lesson that I learned thus early in my experience as a teacher I have never forgotten. In all my work at Tuskegee Institute I have lost no opportunity to impress upon our teachers the importance of training their students to study, analyze, and compare actual things, and to use what they have learned in the school room and in the textbook, to enable them to observe, think about, and deal with the objects and situations of actual life.

Not long ago I visited the class room of a new teacher at Tuskegee, who was conducting a class in measurements. This teacher had insisted that each member of the class should commit to memory the tables of measurement, and when I came in they were engaged in reciting, sing-song, something that sounded like a sort of litany composed of feet, yards, rods, acres, gills, pints, quarts, ounces, pounds, and the rest. I looked on at this proceeding for a few minutes; then a happy

thought occurred to me and I asked the teacher to let me take the class in hand. I began by asking if anyone in the class had ever measured the class room 1ll which they were sitting. There was a dumb silence. Then I asked if anyone had ever marked off an acre of actual land, had ever measured a gill of water, or had ever weighed an ounce or a pound of sugar. Not a hand was raised in reply.

Then I told the teacher that I would like to take charge of the class for a few days. Before the week was over, I had seen to it that every member of the class had supplied himself with a rule or a measure of some sort. Under my direction the students measured the class room and found what it would cost to paint the walls of the room.

From the class room we went to a part of the farm where the students were engaged in planting sweet potatoes. Soon we had an acre of sweet potatoes measured off. We computed the number of bushels raised on that acre and calculated the cost and profit of raising them.

Before the week was over the whole class had been through the boarding department, where they had an opportunity to weigh actual sugar. From the steward we obtained some interesting figures as to how much sugar was used a day; then we computed how much was used by each student. We went to the farm again and weighed a live pig, and I had the class find out the selling price of pork on that particular day, not in Chicago, but in Alabama. I had them calculate the amount that, not an imaginary pig or a pig in Chicago, the pig that they had weighed would bring that day in the local market. It took some time to go through all these operations, but I think that it paid to do so. Besides, it was fun. It was fun for me, and it was a great deal more fun for the students. Incidentally the teacher got an awakening and learned a lesson that I dare say he has never forgotten.

Source: Booker T. Washington, "Chapter 6: A Commencement Oration on Cabbages," *My Larger Education: Chapters From My Experience*, Doubleday and Company Inc, 1911.

Figure 3.1: Source: http://commons.wikimedia.org/wiki/File:Booker_T._Washington.JPG.

Closing Activity

Up to this point, you have experienced using OUR THINK-ING TOOLBOX. To give you this experience, we used several ***strategies for teaching and learning***, which are listed on the following page.

Directions

Select one ***strategy*** from the list on the next page that you think is particularly valuable and then respond to the question that follows:

Strategy: _____

What effect do you think this *strategy* had on you as a learner?

_____

_____

_____

	12 STRATEGIES for TEACHING and LEARNING
1	**Discussion-Oriented Student Seating Strategy** Arrange your students' seating in such a way that the students can comfortably see, hear, and communicate with each other across the classroom.
2	**Name Tents and Randomly Assigned Seating Strategy** Use a "name tent" for each of your students so that you can call them by their names from the first time you see them and seat them randomly every class session.
3	**Use of a Speaker's Voice Strategy** Explain to your students that each time they speak, they should use a strong, clear voice that can be heard by everyone in the classroom.
4	**Popcorn Read Strategy** Let students know that when you say "popcorn read," it means "someone" should read—in a loud, clear voice—the part(s) of the lesson that you have indicated (e.g., a direction, sentence, reading excerpt).
5	**Clear and Complete Sentences (Written and Spoken Thoughts) Strategy** Direct your students to respond to Prompts and extended writing activities using clear and complete sentences (thoughts).
6	**Circulate-to-Guide Strategy** Move around the room to offer suggestions, pointers, and guidance to your students as they work on the lessons in the classroom.

7	**Timed-Activities with Clear, Concise, Written Directions Strategy** Communicate to your students that for every activity there are written directions to follow and a specific amount of time is given in which that activity should be completed.
8	**Zenergy Chime Signal Strategy** Signal your class using a Zenergy Chime to capture their attention when a new phase of an activity is about to begin.
9	**"Call On Students" Strategy** Call on students to share their responses to prompts and to questions you pose spontaneously, rather than asking for volunteers or allowing students to call out answers.
10	**"I Don't Know Yet" Strategy** Tell your students that when you call on them and they don't know the answer, to please pause to reflect and answer, "I don't know yet."
11	**Collaborative Activities Strategy** Cultivate thoughtful discussion by having groups of two or more students work together to discuss and evaluate thoughts that they have written independently, prior to getting together.
12	**Stand Up and Move Strategy** Have your students get out of their seats to move somewhere in the classroom to discuss their responses to prompts.

Homework

Directions

- Read the paragraph from Albert Einstein that appears on the following page.
- Create a dialogue between you and Albert Einstein about how to help students accomplish high-quality learning in the classroom.

Note: This dialogue should be a thoughtful discussion of important ideas. Begin your dialogue with a thought-provoking QUESTION.

You: _____

_____

Einstein: _____

_____

You: _____

_____

Einstein: _____

_____

You: _____

_____

Einstein: _____

_____

Title:

By Albert Einstein

"Sometimes one sees in the school simply the instrument for transferring a certain maximum quantity of knowledge to the growing generation. But that is not right. Knowledge is dead; the school however, serves the living. It should develop in the young individuals those qualities and capabilities which are of value for the welfare of the commonwealth. But that does not mean that individuality should be destroyed and the individual become a mere tool of the community, like a bee or an ant. For a community of standardized individuals without personal originality and personal aims would be a poor community without possibilities for development. On the contrary, the aim must be the training of independently acting and thinking individuals."

Source: Albert Einstein, *Out of My Later Years*, pp. 34-35. Copyright © 1950 by Kensington Publishing Corp. Reprinted with permission.

Figure 3.2: Source: http://commons.wikimedia.org/wiki/File:Einstein1921_by_F_Schmutzer_2.jpg.

Name: _____

Date: _____

Analysis of Book Excerpt *Silent Spring* by Rachel Carson and Video Interview

OA   Quote, Margaret Mead

MA   Book Excerpt, Rachel Carson

CA   Quote, Albert Schweitzer

HW   Video Excerpt, Chris Hedges

"What is worth learning is worth learning well."

—Alfred North Whitehead

Opening Activity

Directions

- Read the quote that follows.
- **PARAPHRASE** this quote by Margaret Mead. In other words, capture exactly what Margaret Mead communicates to us in your own words.

"Never doubt that a small group of thoughtful, committed citizens can change the world. Indeed, it is the only thing that ever has."

—Margaret Mead

_____

_____

_____

_____

_____

Main Activity

Directions

- Read the book excerpt by Rachel Carson that appears on the following pages.
- Respond to the **prompts** that follow in clear and complete sentences.
- Complete a **DOXI** for the word "moribund," which is **bolded** in the reading.

1. What do you think Rachel Carson's **PURPOSE** was for writing this section of her book?

_____

_____

_____

PURPOSE TOOL	<u>R</u> Explain what you think the author wanted to accomplish through this reading.

2. <u>Underline</u> in the text what you think is the most **SIGNIFICANT SENTENCE** in this excerpt. Next, tell **why** you selected this as the most significant sentence.

_____

_____

_____

SIGNIFICANT SENTENCE(S) TOOL	<u>R</u> Select the sentence(s) you think is the most important in the reading and tell why you selected it.

3. Identify the specific **PROBLEM** Rachel Carson is talking about in this book excerpt.

_____

_____

_____

PROBLEM TOOL	**R** Identify the main problem or issue focused on in the reading. Explain why this is a problem.

4. What **QUESTION** would you really like to ask Rachel Carson about the problem she identifies in this book excerpt?

_____

_____

_____

QUESTION TOOL	**R** Pose a thought-provoking question(s) to the author about something that caught your attention in the reading.

5. What do you think was the specific **TOPIC** Rachel Carson focused on in this book excerpt?

_____

_____

_____

TOPIC TOOL	**R** Identify the specific topic that the author has written about.

Silent Spring

Excerpt by Rachel Carson

There was once a town in the heart of America where all life seemed to live in harmony with its surroundings. The town lay in the midst of a checkerboard of prosperous farms, with fields of grain and hillsides of orchards where, in spring, white clouds of bloom drifted above the green fields. In autumn, oak and maple and birch set up a blaze of color that flamed and flickered across a backdrop of pines. Then foxes barked in the hills and deer silently crossed the fields, half hidden in the mists of the fall mornings.

Along the roads, laurel, viburnum and alder, great ferns and wildflowers delighted the traveler's eye through much of the year. Even in winter the roadsides were places of beauty, where countless birds came to feed on the berries and on the seed heads of the dried weeds rising above the snow. The countryside was, in fact, famous for the abundance and variety of its bird life, and when the flood of migrants was pouring through in spring and fall people traveled from great distances to observe them. Others came to fish the streams, which flowed clear and cold out of the hills and contained shady pools where trout lay. So it had been from the days many years ago when the first settlers raised their houses, sank their wells, and built their barns.

Then a strange blight crept over the area and everything began to change. Some evil spell had settled on the community: mysterious maladies swept the flocks of chickens; the cattle and sheep sickened and died. Everywhere was a shadow of death. The farmers spoke of much illness among their families. In the town the doctors had become more and more puzzled by new kinds of sickness appearing among their patients. There had been several sudden and unexplained deaths, not only among adults but even among children, who would be stricken suddenly while at play and die within a few hours.

There was a strange stillness. The birds, for example where had they gone? Many people spoke of them, puzzled and disturbed. The feeding stations in the backyards were deserted. The few birds seen anywhere were **moribund**; they trembled violently and could not fly. It was a spring without voices. On the mornings that had once throbbed with the dawn chorus of robins, catbirds, doves, jays, wrens, and scores of other bird voices there was now no sound; only silence lay over the fields and woods and marsh.

On the farms the hens brooded, but no chicks hatched. The farmers complained that they were unable to raise any pigs the litters were small and the young survived only a few days. The apple trees were coming into bloom but no bees droned among the blossoms, so there was no pollination and there would be no fruit.

The roadsides, once so attractive, were now lined with browned and 249 withered vegetation as though swept by fire. These, too, were silent, deserted by all living things. Even the streams were now lifeless. Anglers no longer visited them, for all the fish had died.

In the gutters under the eaves and between the shingles of the roofs, a white granular powder still showed a few patches; some weeks before it had fallen like snow upon the roofs and the lawns, the fields and streams.

No witchcraft, no enemy action had silenced the rebirth of new life in this stricken world. The people had done it themselves.

This town does not actually exist, but it might easily have a thousand counterparts in America or elsewhere in the world. I know of no community that has experienced all the misfortunes I describe. Yet every one of these disasters has actually happened somewhere, and many real communities have already suffered a substantial number of them. A grim specter has crept upon us almost unnoticed, and this imagined tragedy may easily become a stark reality we all shall know.

Source: Rachel Carson, *Silent Spring*, pp. 1-3. Copyright © 1962 by Houghton Mifflin Harcourt. Reprinted with permission.

Figure 4.1: Source: http://commons.wikimedia.org/wiki/File:Rachel-Carson.jpg.

Moribund

WORD (*Concept*)

D Select the appropriate dictionary **D**efinition (use www.dictionary.com or another dictionary).

_____

_____

O Put this definition into your **O**wn words (i.e., **paraphrase**).

_____

_____

X Give an e**X**ample of this **WORD** (concept) from your own personal experience.

_____

_____

I **I**llustrate the **WORD** (concept) by going to Google Images and finding an image that you think gives the best representation of the meaning of the **WORD** (concept) as you now understand it.

Closing Activity

Directions

- Read the quote that follows.
- Paraphrase this quote by Albert Schweitzer. In other words, capture exactly what Albert Schweitzer communicates to us in your own words.

Figure 4.2: Source: http://commons.wikimedia.org/wiki/File:Albert_Schweitzer_Nobel.jpg.

"Compassion, in which all ethics must take root, can only attain its full breadth and depth if it embraces all living creatures and does not limit itself to mankind."

—Albert Schweitzer

_____

_____

_____

_____

Homewok

Directions

- In the link that follows, watch the video of "The Climate Emergency with Dahr Jamail" from *On Contact with Chris Hedges* (https://www.rt.com/shows/on-contact/452283-alaska-extinction-climate-disruption/).
- Respond to the following **prompts** in clear, complete sentences.

1. What struck you as the most important **PROBLEM** about what was discussed in this video?

_____

_____

_____

2. What is one particular part of this **PROBLEM** that you would like to further investigate? Explain **why**.

_____

_____

_____

_____

_____

3. How would you begin to carry out this investigation?

_____

_____

_____

_____

_____

Investigation Plan (Begin)

OA   Topic

MA   Peer Discussion: Topic, Title, and Problem

CA   Problem, Purpose, and Title

HW   Investigative Article, Part 1—INVESTIGATION PLAN: Draft

"What is worth learning is worth learning well."

—Alfred North Whitehead

Opening Activity

Directions

- Review the three topics that follow and respond to the questions that follow.

  - "Health"

  - "Children's Health"

  - "Children's Health Problems and Peer Nutrition"

1. Describe how these three topics are different.

   _____

   _____

   _____

2. Which of the three topics above will be most practical to investigate and write about? Explain **why** you say this.

   _____

   _____

   _____

Main Activity

You will write an **Investigative Article** over the next ten class sessions. This article will consist of three parts: **INVESTIGATION PLAN, INVESTIGATION RESEARCH**, and **INVESTIGATION FINDINGS**.

Our work will now focus on your **INVESTIGATION PLAN**.

Directions

▪ Based on what we learned in the "Opening Activity," identify and write one "specific" **TOPIC** in either **education** <u>or</u> **social issues** (from Classes #1–#4) that you would be interested in investigating and writing about.

▪ Review the **TOPIC** Tool (the "<u>W</u>" version) as you prepare to investigate the "specific" **TOPIC** you chose.

Write what will be the "specific" **TOPIC** of focus for your investigation:

_____

_____

TOPIC TOOL	<u>W</u> Select a specific topic to be the focus of your writing.

Use the four criteria that follow to review the "specific **TOPIC**" your partner came up with. Then have a "peer discussion" with your partner to give recommendations to help one another make the "specific" **TOPIC** clear, focused, important, and practical:

Criteria (for Peer Discussion)

➤ Clear: Does the **TOPIC** make clear what is to be investigated?

➤ Focused: Is the **TOPIC** as focused ("specific") as it needs to be?

➤ Important: Is there a need to investigate this **TOPIC**?

➤ Practical: Is this investigation practical to complete in the given time frame?

"Peer Discussion"

Peer Ideas (Recommendation)

Rewrite your partner's **TOPIC** in light of these four criteria:

_____

_____

_____

As a final step, rewrite the **TOPIC** you will investigate:

_____

_____

_____

Closing Activity

Directions

- To prepare to write your **INVESTIGATION PLAN** for the "specific" topic you chose, respond to the **prompts** that follow.

1. The specific **TOPIC** I will focus on is:

_____

2. The main **PROBLEM** I will focus on in my investigation is:

_____

_____

I think this is an important **PROBLEM** to investigate because ...

_____

_____

_____

PROBLEM TOOL	**W** Identify the main problem or issue that is the focus of your writing. Explain why this is a problem.

3. The **PURPOSE** for my investigation is:

_____

_____

_____

PURPOSE TOOL	<u>W</u> Explain what you want to accomplish through your writing.

4. The "Working" **TITLE** for my investigation is:

_____

TITLE TOOL	<u>W</u> Create a title that expresses the main idea (focus) of your writing.

Homework

Directions

- Fill in the chart below with your ideas for your "working" **INVESTIGATION PLAN** to be reviewed at our next class meeting.

- To do this, use what you came up with today and then make any further adjustments you think are needed to make the wording even better.

My "Working" **INVESTIGATION PLAN** Ideas

TOPIC	
TITLE	
PROBLEM	
PURPOSE	

Investigation Plan (Continued)

OA Question Creation

MA INVESTIGATION PLAN: Begin Draft

CA LAB: Information/Review of Literature

HW INVESTIGATION PLAN: Continue Draft

"What is worth learning is worth learning well."

—Alfred North Whitehead

Opening Activity

Directions

- Complete the following sentence in your own words.

    A **quest** is _____

- Review the **QUESTION** Tool (the "<u>W</u>" version) that follows to create two key **QUESTIONS** you will use to focus on in your investigation.

*Note: Consider turning the "working" **TITLE** you created in Class #5 into the form of a question.*

QUESTION TOOL	<u>W</u> Pose a thought-provoking question(s) you will investigate and address in your writing.

TWO KEY QUESTIONS	Q#1:
	Q#2:

Main Activity

Directions

▪ Use the two **criteria** that follow to make recommendations about the **QUES-TIONS** your partner posed.

Criteria (for Peer Discussion)
➢ Focused: Do your **QUESTIONS** help keep your focus on what to look for?
➢ Practical: Can the search for **INFORMATION** to address and answer these QUESTIONS be done in a reasonable amount of time?

"Peer Discussion"

TWO KEY QUESTIONS (Peer Recommendations)	Q#1:
	Q#2:

▪ Revise your **QUESTIONS** based on the recommendations you received from your partner and the class discussion.

Revised Questions

TWO KEY QUESTIONS (Revised)	Q#1:
	Q#2:

Directions

- Add your revised **QUESTIONS** to the chart that follows.

- Use what you have on your chart to guide you as we go to the LAB to write a draft of your **INVESTIGATION PLAN**.

MY "Working" **INVESTIGATION PLAN** Ideas

TOPIC	
TITLE	
PROBLEM	
PURPOSE	
QUESTIONS	

Closing Activity (in LAB)

Directions

- Create a Word document (double-spaced) as shown in the setup that follows to write a draft of your **INVESTIGATION PLAN**.

- Use the directions in parentheses to guide your thoughts for each <u>subsection</u> (e.g., **TOPIC, PROBLEM**).

Note: <u>Subsections</u> provide the structure to follow as you write your paper.

<u>Investigative Article</u>, Part 1—INVESTIGATION PLAN

TITLE
(Make sure your "working" **TITLE** expresses to readers exactly what your investigation is about.)

TOPIC

(State the "specific" **TOPIC** you will investigate and elaborate to let us know why you chose this as the focus of your investigation.)

PROBLEM

(State the **PROBLEM** you will investigate, provide some background about the **PROBLEM**, and make the case for why this needs to be investigated.)

PURPOSE

(State your **PURPOSE** for carrying out this investigation and make clear the importance of what you think you will accomplish through this investigation.)

QUESTION

(State the two **QUESTIONS** you posed for your investigation. Identify sources you think you will look at for information to answer these questions.)

Homework

Directions

- Continue to write the draft of your **INVESTIGATION PLAN** in the Word document (double-spaced) you created in class today.

Note: The final version will be handed in at the beginning of Class #8.

- Use the directions in parentheses to guide your thoughts for each <u>subsection</u>.

<u>Investigative Article</u>, Part 1—INVESTIGATION PLAN

TITLE

(Make sure your "working" **TITLE** expresses to readers exactly what your investigation is about.)

TOPIC

(State the "specific" **TOPIC** you will investigate and elaborate to let us know why you chose this as the focus of your investigation.)

PROBLEM

(State the **PROBLEM** you will investigate, provide some background about the **PROBLEM**, and make the case for why this needs to be investigated.)

PURPOSE

(State your **PURPOSE** for carrying out this investigation and make clear the importance of what you think you will accomplish through this investigation.)

QUESTION

(State the two **QUESTIONS** you posed for your investigation. Identify sources you think you will look at for information to answer these questions.)

CLASS #7

Investigation Plan (Continued) and Investigation Research (Begin)

OA   INVESTIGATION PLAN: Peer Recommendations

MA   Significant Sentences

CA   Information/Review of Literature (Research)

HW   INVESTIGATION PLAN: Finalize to Submit in Class #8

"What is worth learning is worth learning well."

—Alfred North Whitehead

Opening Activity

Directions

- Read your partner's draft of the **INVESTIGATION PLAN** and give your recommendations for each <u>subsection</u> that follows.

<u>Partner</u>

✓ **TOPIC:**

(*State the "specific" **TOPIC** you will investigate and elaborate to let us know **why** you chose this as the focus of your investigation.)

<u>Recommendations</u>:

_____

_____

_____

✓ **PROBLEM:**

(State the **PROBLEM** you will investigate, provide some background about the **PROBLEM**, and make the case for **why** this needs to be investigated.)

<u>Recommendations</u>:

_____

_____

_____

✓ **PURPOSE:**

(State your **PURPOSE** for carrying out this investigation and make clear the importance of what you think you will accomplish through this investigation.)

Recommendations:

_____

_____

_____

✓ **QUESTIONS:**

(State the two **QUESTIONS** you posed for your investigation. Identify sources you think you will look at for information to answer these questions.)

Recommendations:

_____

_____

_____

✓ **TITLE:**

(Make sure your **TITLE** expresses exactly what your investigation is about.)

Recommendations:

_____

_____

_____

Directions

- Discuss your recommendations with your partner.

- Use these recommendations as appropriate to edit your **INVESTIGATION PLAN** and submit your final version at the Class #8 meeting.

Main Activity

Directions

- Review the **SIGNIFICANT SENTENCE** Tool (the "<u>W</u>" version) and then respond to the **prompt** that follows.

SIGNIFICANT SENTENCE(S) TOOL	<u>W</u> Create sentences that express your thoughts and are important to accomplish the purpose of your writing. Elaborate and give examples to make your thoughts clear.

PROMPT: Revise what you have written for the **PROBLEM** <u>subsection</u> of your **INVESTIGATION PLAN** through the use of the **SIGNIFICANT SENTENCE** Tool. Elaborate with a few examples that you have read or heard about or experienced to illustrate the reality and seriousness of the **PROBLEM** you have chosen to investigate.

PROBLEM (revised)

_____

_____

_____

_____

_____

_____

_____

_____

Closing Activity

Directions

- If you were asked to give a name to the next tool you will use to carry out your investigation, what would the name of this tool be?

_____ **TOOL**

Why?

_____

_____

_____

Directions

- Review the **INFORMATION/REVIEW of LITERATURE** Tool (the "<u>W</u>" version).

INFORMATION/ REVIEW OF LITERATURE TOOL	<u>W</u> Search for information and ideas to deepen your understanding and support important points you make in your writing. Cite relevant sources accordingly.

- Identify specific **INFORMATION** you think you will need for your investigation. Name <u>two</u> **sources** you will go to for this **INFORMATION** and explain **why** you will look at those sources.

INFORMATION (**what** you search for): _____

_____

_____

_____

_____

_____

_____

Source #1 (**where** you will look): _____

_____

_____

_____

Why will you look there: _____

_____

_____

Source #2 (where you will look): _____

_____

_____

_____

Why will you look there: _____

_____

_____

_____

Homework

Directions

- Finalize your **INVESTIGATION PLAN** for submission at the beginning of Class #8.

Investigative Article, Part 1—INVESTIGATION PLAN

TITLE

(Make sure your "working" **TITLE** expresses to readers exactly what your investigation is about.)

TOPIC

(State the "specific" **TOPIC** you will investigate and elaborate to let us know why you chose this as the focus of your investigation.)

PROBLEM

(State the **PROBLEM** you will investigate, provide some background about the **PROBLEM**, and make the case for why this needs to be investigated.)

PURPOSE

(State your **PURPOSE** for carrying out this investigation and make clear the importance of what you think you will accomplish through this investigation.)

QUESTION

(State the two **QUESTIONS** you posed for your investigation. Identify sources you think you will look at for information to answer these questions.)

Investigation Research (Continued)

INVESTIGATION PLAN—Submit Today

OA   INVESTIGATION RESEARCH: Structure

MA   Speak in the Author's Voice, Paraphrase, and Source Notes

CA   LAB: Begin Research

HW   Investigative Article, Part 2—INVESTIGATION RESEARCH

"What is worth learning is worth learning well."

—Alfred North Whitehead

Opening Activity

Directions

- The five tools used so far became the <u>subsections</u> for our **INVESTIGATION PLAN.** This gives us a structure to follow as we write.

- Under "**INVESTIGATION RESEARCH**," write one or a few words next to each bullet for what you think the name should be of the <u>subsections </u>of this phase of the investigation.

Investigation Plan

- TITLE
- TOPIC
- PROBLEM
- PURPOSE
- QUESTIONS

Investigation Research

- _____
- _____
- _____
- _____

Directions

- Review the list of <u>subsections</u> to use for our **INVESTIGATION RESEARCH.**
- In a clear, complete sentence, explain **why** you think each <u>subsection</u> will be important to research and write about.

Investigation Research

- **Background and Significance of the PROBLEM**

Why? _____

_____

_____

_____

- **Causes of the PROBLEM**

Why?_____

_____

_____

_____

- **Solutions to the PROBLEM**

Why? _____

_____

_____

_____

■ **Roadblocks to Overcoming the PROBLEM**

Why? _____

_____

_____

_____

Main Activity

Directions

▪ Review the **SPEAK in the AUTHOR'S VOICE** Tool (the <u>W</u> version) and briefly describe how you think using this tool will help you carry out your investigation.

_____

_____

_____

_____

SPEAK IN THE AUTHOR'S VOICE TOOL	<u>W</u> Include quotes (or paraphrases of quotes) from selected authors or sources to support and clarify what you want to express in your writing. Cite relevant sources accordingly.

▪ Review the **PARAPHRASE** Tool (the <u>W</u> version) and briefly describe why you would sometimes use this tool instead of a direct quote in your writing.

_____

_____

_____

_____

PARAPHRASE TOOL	<u>W</u> Paraphrase a sentence(s) from what you read to use in your writing.

Directions

▪ How would you respond if a friend asks you, "What are two things I should do to take good notes from the sources I find for my investigation?"

_____

_____

_____

Directions

▪ Review the "source notes" form on the following page as a way to take and organize notes from the sources you find.

▪ Review its three main features: "**Bibliographic Information**," "**Pg(s)/Para(s)/Line(s)**," and "**Notes (Direct Quotes or Paraphrases)/My Comments and Ideas**."

▪ Choose **one** of these three features and explain how you think this will help you as you take notes from sources you find.

Feature: _____

How it will help:_____

_____

_____

_____

_____

_____

Source Notes

For: _____

Bibliographic Information		Date Notes Taken: _____	
Author(s): _____			
Name of Book, Article, Website, (& URL):			
_____			
Page(s): _____			
Publication Date: _____		City, State: _____	
Publisher: _____			

Pg(s)	Para(s)	Line(s)	Notes (Direct Quotes or Paraphrases)/My Comments and Ideas

Directions

- Read the following descriptions of how to best use each of the three main features of this method for taking source notes.

1. **Bibliographic Information**

   While you are at a particular source (i.e., book, article, website/URL), copy the information that is asked for. This will make sure you can **a)** easily locate this source again and **b)** have what you need for your "References" (or "Work Cited") page. **See NOTE #1**.

2. **Pg(s)/Para(s)/Line(s)**

   Note the exact location in **each source** (i.e., specific pages, paragraphs, and lines) for the direct quotes, paraphrases of quotes, and general references to be able to get right back to this information whenever you need to.

3. **Notes (Direct Quotes or Paraphrases)/My Comments and Ideas**

   Notes:

   Copy the exact notes you want to use in your writing and make clear which are exact quotations (use quotation marks on these) and which are your paraphrases of quotations. **See NOTE #2**.

   My Comments and Ideas:

   Write your thoughts about these specific notes or your own original ideas that this information brings to mind.

NOTE #1: To create your "References" (or "Work Cited") page, use the **bibliographic information** you have written down on the **source notes** forms and then use the format style (e.g., *Modern Language Association* [*MLA*], *American Psychological Association* [*APA*], *The Chicago Manual of Style* [*Chicago*]) you are required to follow.

NOTE #2: To use quotations and your paraphrases of quotations in your writing, use the format style (e.g., *MLA*, *APA*, *Chicago*) you are required to follow. Directions

- Review the example of how these three main features can be used to take source notes from the Rachel Carson book excerpt (*Silent Spring*) we read in Class #4.

Source Notes

For: _____

Bibliographic Information	Date Notes Taken: _____

Author(s): *Rachel Carson*
Name of Book, Article, Website, (& URL): *Silent Spring*
Page(s): *?*_____
Publication Date: *1962*_____ City, State: *New York, NY*_____
Publisher: *Houghton Mifflin*_____

Pg(s)	Para(s)	Line(s)	Notes (Direct Quotes or Paraphrases)/My Comments and Ideas
2	*2*	*5–7*	*Author:* *"The farmers spoke of much illness among their families. In the town the doctors had become more and more puzzled by new kinds of sickness appearing among their patients."*
2	*2*	*5–7*	*My Comment:* *This quote demonstrates how important it is for people to understand that pollution of the environment kills people and destroys lives.*
2	*2*	*5–7*	*My Idea:* *This makes me want to investigate and find out what one of the main causes of environmental pollution is and to find some of the best solutions to overcome this pollution.*

Closing Activity (in LAB)

Directions

- Use the **INFORMATION/REVIEW OF LITERATURE** Tool to carry out research for your investigation.

INFORMATION/ REVIEW OF LITERATURE TOOL	**W** Search for information and ideas to deepen your understanding and support important points you make in your writing. Cite relevant sources accordingly.

- Find two relevant sources that have valuable information to help you write the first <u>subsection</u> of your **INVESTIGATION RESEARCH: Background and Significance of the PROBLEM**.

- Complete a "source notes" form for **each source** you find. Write the specific information you think you will use for this <u>subsection</u>.

Source Notes #1

For: Background and Significance of the PROBLEM

Bibliographic Information Date Notes Taken: _____

Author(s): _____

Name of Book, Article, Website, (& URL):

_____

Page(s): _____

Publication Date: _____   City, State: _____

Publisher: _____

Pg(s)	Para(s)	Line(s)	Notes (Direct Quotes or Paraphrases)/My Comments and Ideas

Source Notes #2

For: Background and Significance of the PROBLEM

Bibliographic Information Date Notes Taken: _____

Author(s): _____

Name of Book, Article, Website, (& URL):

_____

Page(s): _____

Publication Date: _____ City, State: _____

Publisher: _____

Pg(s)	Para(s)	Line(s)	Notes (Direct Quotes or Paraphrases)/My Comments and Ideas

Homewor k

Directions

- Use the **INFORMATION/REVIEW OF LITERATURE** Tool to carry out research for your investigation.

- Find one more relevant source in addition to the two you found in the LAB today for the first <u>subsection</u> of your **INVESTIGATION RESEARCH: Background and Significance of the PROBLEM**.

- Complete a "source notes" form for **each source** you find.

Source Notes #3

For: Background and Significance of the PROBLEM

Bibliographic Information	Date Notes Taken: _____
Author(s): _____	
Name of Book, Article, Website, (& URL):	
_____	
Page(s): _____	
Publication Date: _____	City, State: _____
Publisher: _____	

Pg(s)	Para(s)	Line(s)	Notes (Direct Quotes or Paraphrases)/My Comments and Ideas

Directions

- Find three relevant sources for the second <u>subsection</u> of your **INVESTIGATION RESEARCH: Causes of the PROBLEM**.

- Complete a "source notes" form for **each source** you find.

Source Notes #1

For: Causes of the PROBLEM

Bibliographic Information   Date Notes Taken: _____
Author(s): _____
Name of Book, Article, Website, (& URL):
_____
Page(s): _____
Publication Date: _____   City, State: _____
Publisher: _____

Pg(s)	Para(s)	Line(s)	Notes (Direct Quotes or Paraphrases)/My Comments and Ideas

Source Notes #2

For: Causes of the PROBLEM

| **Bibliographic Information** | Date Notes Taken: _____ |

Author(s): _____

Name of Book, Article, Website, (& URL):

_____

Page(s): _____

Publication Date: _____ City, State: _____

Publisher: _____

Pg(s)	Para(s)	Line(s)	Notes (Direct Quotes or Paraphrases)/My Comments and Ideas

Source Notes #3

For: Causes of the PROBLEM

Bibliographic Information	Date Notes Taken: _____
Author(s): _____	
Name of Book, Article, Website, (& URL):	
_____	
Page(s): _____	
Publication Date: _____	City, State: _____
Publisher: _____	

Pg(s)	Para(s)	Line(s)	Notes (Direct Quotes or Paraphrases)/My Comments and Ideas

Name: _____

Date: _____

Investigation Research (Continued)

OA   Peer Discussion: Source Notes (Review and Recommend)

MA   Peer Discussion: Source Notes (Discuss and Revise)

CA   LAB: INVESTIGATION RESEARCH: Begin Draft of "Background" and "Causes" Subsections

HW   INVESTIGATION RESEARCH: Continue Draft of "Background" and "Causes" Subsections

"What is worth learning is worth learning well."

—Alfred North Whitehead

Opening and Main Activity

Directions

- Use the three criteria that follow to review your partner's "source notes" (**Notes/My Comments and Ideas**) for the "**Background and Significance of the PROBLEM**" and the "**Causes of the PROBLEM**" subsections of their **INVESTIGATION PLAN**.

Criteria (for Peer Discussion)

➢ Clear: Are the **"Notes/My Comments and Ideas"** clearly understandable?

➢ Focused: Are the **"Notes/My Comments and Ideas"** as focused ("specific") as they need to be?

➢ Important: Are the **"Notes/My Comments and Ideas"** important to the PROBLEM investigated?

- Give recommendations to your partner concerning the "sources" and the "information" he or she found.

- Discuss your recommendations with your partner and then revise your "source notes" accordingly.

"Peer Discussion"

Background and Significance of the PROBLEM
Source #1

✓ <u>Recommendations</u> on the value of **Information:**

_____

_____

_____

_____

✓ <u>Recommendations</u> on the value of **Source:**

_____

_____

_____

Source #2

✓ <u>Recommendations</u> on the value of **Information:**

_____

_____

_____

_____

✓ <u>Recommendations</u> on the value of **Source:**

_____

_____

_____

Source #3

✓ <u>Recommendations</u> on the value of **Information:**

_____

_____

_____

✓ <u>Recommendations</u> on the value of **Source:**

_____

_____

_____

Causes of the PROBLEM
Source #1

✓ <u>Recommendations</u> on the value of **Information:**

_____

_____

_____

✓ <u>Recommendations</u> on the value of **Source:**

_____

_____

_____

Source #2

✓ <u>Recommendations</u> on the value of **Information:**

_____

_____

_____

✓ <u>Recommendations</u> on the value of **Source:**

_____

_____

_____

Source #3

✓ <u>Recommendations</u> on the value of **Information:**

_____

_____

_____

✓ <u>Recommendations</u> on the value of **Source:**

_____

_____

_____

Closing Activity (in LAB)

Directions

- Create a Word document (double-spaced) as shown in the setup that follows to write a draft of your **Investigative Article**, Part 2—**INVESTIGATIVE RESEARCH**.

- Use the information you found in your research, along with your own thoughts, to write each <u>subsection</u>.

Note: <u>Subsections</u> provide the structure to follow as you write your paper.

<u>Investigative Article</u>, Part 2—<u>INVESTIGATIVE RESEARCH</u>

Background and Significance of the PROBLEM

Causes of the PROBLEM

Homework

Directions

- Continue to write the draft of your **INVESTIGATIVE RESEARCH** in the Word document (double-spaced) you created in class today.

Note: You will submit the final version at the beginning of Class #12.

Name: _____

Date: _____

Investigation Research (Continued)

OA Peer Discussion: Draft of "Background" and "Causes" Subsections

MA LAB: Begin Research on "Solutions" and "Roadblocks" Subsections

CA LAB: Continue Research on "Solutions" and "Roadblocks" Subsections

HW INVESTIGATION RESEARCH: Continue Draft of "Background" and "Causes" Subsections/Add Draft of "Solutions" and "Roadblocks" Subsections

"What is worth learning is worth learning well."

—Alfred North Whitehead

Opening Activity

Directions

- Have a "peer discussion" with your partner to give recommendations about your partner's draft (Word document) of the **"Background"** and the **"Causes"** subsections of their **INVESTIGATION RESEARCH**.

- Make recommendations to your partner concerning the draft of his or her **"Introduction"** and **"Causes"** subsections in the space provided next.

- Discuss your recommendations with your partner.

- Review and consider your partner's recommendations for possible use as you continue to draft and edit these two subsections.

"Peer Discussion"

✓ Background and Significance of the PROBLEM
Recommendations:

_____

_____

_____

_____

✓ Causes of the PROBLEM
Recommendations:

_____

_____

_____

_____

Main Activity and
Closing Activity (in LAB)

Directions

- Use the **INFORMATION/REVIEW OF LITERATURE** Tool to find three relevant sources for the third and the fourth <u>subsections</u> of your **INVESTIGATIVE RESEARCH: Solutions to PROBLEM and Roadblocks to Overcoming the PROBLEM**.

INFORMATION/ REVIEW OF LITERATURE TOOL	<u>**W**</u> Search for information and ideas to deepen your understanding and support important points you make in your writing. Cite relevant sources accordingly.

- Complete a "source notes" form for **each source** you find. Write the specific information you think you will use for this <u>subsection</u>.

Source Notes #1

For: Solutions to PROBLEM

Bibliographic Information	Date Notes Taken: _____

Author(s): _____

Name of Book, Article, Website, (& URL):

_____

Page(s): _____

Publication Date: _____   City, State: _____

Publisher: _____

Pg(s)	Para(s)	Line(s)	Notes (Direct Quotes or Paraphrases)/My Comments and Ideas

Source Notes #2

For: Solutions to PROBLEM

Bibliographic Information	Date Notes Taken: _____

Author(s): _____

Name of Book, Article, Website, (& URL):

_____

Page(s): _____

Publication Date: _____ City, State: _____

Publisher: _____

Pg(s)	Para(s)	Line(s)	Notes (Direct Quotes or Paraphrases)/My Comments and Ideas

Source Notes #3

For: Solutions to PROBLEM

Bibliographic Information	Date Notes Taken: _____
Author(s): _____	
Name of Book, Article, Website, (& URL):	
_____	
Page(s): _____	
Publication Date: _____	City, State: _____
Publisher: _____	

Pg(s)	Para(s)	Line(s)	Notes (Direct Quotes or Paraphrases)/My Comments and Ideas

Source Notes #1

For: Roadblocks to Overcoming the PROBLEM

Bibliographic Information	Date Notes Taken: _____

Author(s): _____

Name of Book, Article, Website, (& URL):

_____

Page(s): _____

Publication Date: _____   City, State: _____

Publisher: _____

Pg(s)	Para(s)	Line(s)	**Notes (Direct Quotes or Paraphrases)/My Comments and Ideas**

Source Notes #2

For: Roadblocks to Overcoming the PROBLEM

Bibliographic Information			Date Notes Taken: _____

Author(s): _____

Name of Book, Article, Website, (& URL):

_____

Page(s): _____

Publication Date: _____   City, State: _____

Publisher: _____

Pg(s)	Para(s)	Line(s)	Notes (Direct Quotes or Paraphrases)/My Comments and Ideas

Source Notes #3

For: Roadblocks to Overcoming the PROBLEM

Bibliographic Information Date Notes Taken: _____
Author(s): _____
Name of Book, Article, Website, (& URL):
_____
Page(s): _____
Publication Date:_____   City, State: _____
Publisher: _____

Pg(s)	Para(s)	Line(s)	Notes (Direct Quotes or Paraphrases)/My Comments and Ideas

Homework

Directions

- Continue to write the draft of your **INVESTIGATIVE RESEARCH** by adding the **"Solutions"** and the **"Roadblocks"** <u>subsections</u> to the Word document (double-spaced) you have created.

- Use the information you found in your research, along with your own thoughts, to write each <u>subsection</u>.

Note: You will submit the final version at the beginning of Class #12.

<u>**Investigative Article,** Part 2—**INVESTIGATIVE RESEARCH**</u>
TITLE

Background and Significance of the PROBLEM

Causes of the PROBLEM

Solutions to the PROBLEM

Roadblocks to Overcoming the PROBLEM

Class Investigation Research (Continued) and Investigation Findings (Begin)

OA   Peer Discussion: Draft of "Solutions" and "Roadblocks" Subsections

MA   INVESTIGATION FINDINGS

CA   LAB: Revise Draft of "Solutions" and "Roadblocks" Subsections

HW   INVESTIGATION RESEARCH: Finalize to Submit in Class #12

"What is worth learning is worth learning well."

—Alfred North Whitehead

Opening Activity

Directions

- Have a "peer discussion" with your partner to give recommendations about your partner's draft (Word document) of the **"Solutions"** and the **"Roadblocks"** subsections of his or her **INVESTIGATION RESEARCH**.

- Make recommendations to your partner concerning the draft of his or her **"Solutions"** and the **"Roadblocks"** subsections in the space provided next.

- Discuss your recommendations with your partner.

- Review and consider your partners' recommendations for possible use as you continue to draft and edit these two subsections.

"Peer Discussion"

✓ **Solutions to the PROBLEM**

Recommendations:

_____

_____

_____

_____

✓ Roadblocks to Overcoming the PROBLEM

<u>Recommendations</u>:

_____

_____

_____

_____

Main Activity

Directions

- Review the **CONCLUSION** Tool (the <u>W</u> version) and write one of the most important conclusions you reached about the specific PROBLEM as a result of your investigation. Be sure to explain **how** you reached this **CONCLUSION**.

CONCLUSION TOOL	<u>W</u> State the most important conclusion that you come to in your writing and explain how you reached that conclusion.

CONCLUSION #1

_____

_____

_____

_____

_____

- Review the **RECOMMENDATION** Tool (the <u>W</u> version) and write one **RECOMMENDATION** for what should be done in light of the CONCLUSION you stated earlier.

RECOMMENDATION TOOL	<u>W</u> State what you think should be done to deal effectively with the main problem or issue you address in your writing.

RECOMMENDATION #1

_____

_____

_____

_____

_____

* Review the **CONSEQUENCES** Tool (the **W** version) and state one thing you think will happen if we <u>do follow</u> the RECOMMENDATION you made earlier and one thing that will happen if we <u>do not</u> follow this RECOMMENDATION.

CONSEQUENCES TOOL	**W** State what you think could happen if we follow or do not follow what you recommend or imply in your writing.

CONSEQUENCES

_____

_____

_____

_____

_____

> **CONCLUSIONS, RECOMMENDATIONS,** and **CONSEQUENCES** will be the three subsections for the last part of your **Investigative Article, INVESTIGATION FINDINGS.**

Closing Activity (in LAB)

Directions

- Revise the "**Solutions**" and "**Roadblocks**" <u>subsections</u> in preparation to finalize your **INVESTIGATION RESEARCH** to submit at the beginning of the next class, Class #12.

Homework

Directions

- Finalize your **INVESTIGATION RESEARCH** to submit at the beginning of Class #12.

Investigative Article, Part 2—INVESTIGATIVE RESEARCH

TITLE

Background and Significance of the PROBLEM

Causes of the PROBLEM

Solutions to the PROBLEM

Roadblocks to Overcoming the PROBLEM

Investigation Findings (Continued)

INVESTIGATION RESEARCH—Submit Today

OA INVESTIGATION FINDINGS: Structure

MA LAB: INVESTIGATION FINDINGS: Begin Draft

CA LAB: Peer Discussion: Draft of "Conclusions," "Recommendations," and "Consequences" Subsections

HW Investigative Article, Part 3—INVESTIGATION FINDINGS: Draft

"What is worth learning is worth learning well."

—Alfred North Whitehead

Opening Activity

At this point, you have created an **INVESTIGATION PLAN** that focused on a specific PROBLEM and looked into this through your **INVESTIGATION RESEARCH**.

To complete your **Investigative Article**, you will write about what you found and what you think this means. This will be your **INVESTIGATION FINDINGS**.

Directions

- Use the **CONCLUSION** Tool (the <u>W</u> version) to write one more important conclusion in addition to the one you reached during the last class.

CONCLUSION TOOL	<u>W</u> State the most important conclusion that you come to in your writing and explain how you reached that conclusion.

CONCLUSION #2

_____

_____

_____

_____

_____

- Use the **RECOMMENDATION** Tool (the <u>W</u> version) to write one more recommendation in addition to the one you gave during the last class.

RECOMMENDATION TOOL	<u>W</u> State what you think should be done to deal effectively with the main problem or issue you address in your writing.

RECOMMENDATION #2

_____

_____

_____

_____

_____

- Use the **CONSEQUENCES** Tool (the <u>W</u> version) to elaborate further on what you wrote in the last class about what you think will happen if we do follow your recommendations <u>or</u> if we do not follow your recommendations.

CONSEQUENCES TOOL	<u>W</u> State what you think could happen if we follow or do not follow what you recommend or imply in your writing.

CONSEQUENCES

_____

_____

_____

_____

_____

Main Activity (in LAB)

Directions

- Create a Word document (double-spaced) as shown in the setup that follows to write a draft of your **Investigative Article**, Part 3—**INVESTIGATIVE FINDINGS**.

- Use what you have already written for **CONCLUSIONS, RECOMMENDATIONS**, and **CONSEQUENCES** for these subsections.

Note: Subsections provide the structure to follow as you write your paper.

Investigative Article, Part 3—**INVESTIGATIVE FINDINGS**

CONCLUSIONS

RECOMMENDATIONS

CONSEQUENCES

Closing Activity (in LAB)

Directions

■ Have a "peer discussion" with your partner to give recommendations about your partner's draft (Word document) of the **"CONCLUSIONS,"** **"RECOMMENDATIONS,"** and **"CONSEQUENCES"** <u>subsections</u> of his or her **INVESTIGATION FINDINGS**.

■ Discuss your recommendations with your partner.

■ Review and consider your partners' recommendations for possible use as you continue to draft and edit these three <u>subsections</u>.

<u>"Peer Discussion"</u>

✓ CONCLUSIONS
<u>Recommendations</u>:

_____

_____

_____

_____

✓ RECOMMENDATIONS
<u>Recommendations</u>:

_____

_____

_____

_____

✓ CONSEQUENCES

<u>Recommendations</u>:

_____

_____

_____

_____

Homework

Directions

- Continue to write the draft of your **INVESTIGATIVE FINDINGS** in the Word document (double-spaced) you created in class today.

Note: You will submit the final version at the beginning of Class #14.

Investigation Findings (Continued)

OA   Peer Discussion: Draft of INVESTIGATION FINDINGS

MA   Preparation of Abstract for Presentation

CA   LAB: Revise Draft of INVESTIGATION FINDINGS

HW   **INVESTIGATION FINDINGS**: Finalize to Submit in Class #14/Create
Abstract to Present

*"What is worth learning is
worth learning well."*

—Alfred North Whitehead

Opening Activity

Directions

- Have a "peer discussion" with your partner to read and give your ideas about your partner's draft of each <u>subsection</u> for his or her INVESTIGATION FINDINGS in the space provided next.

- Discuss your ideas with your partner.

- Review and consider your partner's ideas for possible use as you continue to edit and finalize these three <u>subsections</u> of your INVESTIGATION FINDINGS.

CONCLUSIONS

Idea(s) to Consider:

_____

_____

_____

_____

_____

RECOMMENDATIONS

Idea(s) to Consider:

_____

_____

_____

_____

_____

_____

CONSEQUENCES

Idea(s) to Consider:

_____

_____

_____

_____

_____

Main Activity

Directions

- At our next class meeting (Class #14), you will submit your INVESTIGATION FINDINGS and an "abstract" of your **INVESTIGATIVE Article**.

- Create a Word document as shown in the setup that follows to write the _one-page_ "abstract" of your **INVESTIGATIVE Article.**

- You will briefly (three minutes maximum) present your "abstract" to the class using the document camera.

Name: _____

INVESTIGATIVE Article—ABSTRACT

TITLE

Specific **PROBLEM** Investigated

_____

_____

_____

_____

_____

_____

_____

Most Important **CONCLUSIONS** Reached

_____

_____

_____

_____

_____

_____

Most Important **RECOMMENDATIONS**

_____

_____

_____

_____

_____

_____

Closing Activity (in LAB)

Directions

- Continue to work on your INVESTIGATIVE FINDINGS.
- Create your one-page "abstract."

Homework

Directions

Finalize your INVESTIGATION FINDINGS for submission and your "abstract" for presentation for Class #14.

Name: _____

Date: _____

Investigative Article: Abstract Presentations

INVESTIGATION FINDINGS—Submit Today

OA PRESENTATIONS

MA PRESENTATIONS

CA PRESENTATIONS

HW Think About Questions Posed

"What is worth learning is worth learning well."

—Alfred North Whitehead

Opening, Main, and Closing Activities

Directions

- Present the "abstract" of your **Investigative Article** (three minutes maximum).
- Next, write a thought-provoking question that comes to your mind that you would really like an answer to for four of the presentations (include the name of the presenter with your question).

Question:

_____

_____

_____

       (presenter #1: _____)

Question:

_____

_____

_____

       (presenter #2: _____)

Question:

_____

_____

_____

    (presenter #3: _____)

Question:

_____

_____

_____

    (presenter #4: _____)

Homework

Directions

- Think about the questions your classmates posed for your investigation.

- Put the Word documents you created for your INVESTIGATION PLAN, INVESTIGATION RESEARCH, and INVESTIGATION FINDINGS into a single Word document. This will be your **Investigative Article** and submit.

HISTORY
AND
PHILOSOPHY

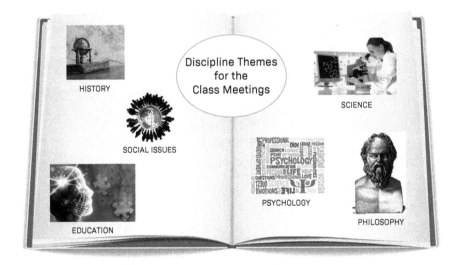

HISTORY

SOCIAL ISSUES

EDUCATION

Discipline Themes
for the
Class Meetings

SCIENCE

PSYCHOLOGY

PHILOSOPHY

Analysis of Book Excerpt *A People's History of the United States* and Opinion Paper

OA Ethiopian Proverb

MA Book Excerpt, Howard Zinn

CA Quotes, Albert Einstein and Booker T. Washington

HW Opinion Paper

"What is worth learning is worth learning well."

—Alfred North Whitehead

Opening Activity

Directions

- **PARAPHRASE** the following quote.
- Respond to the prompt that follows.

"Until lions have their own historians, the hunter will always be glorified."

—Ethiopian Proverb

_____

_____

_____

What would be the **CONSEQUENCE** if the lion got to tell the story, and not the hunter?

_____

_____

_____

Main Activity

Directions

- Read the book excerpt about Christopher Columbus.
  *Note: The words in **bold** come directly from his log (diary).*
- Respond to the prompts that follow in clear and complete sentences.

1. Select what you think is the most **SIGNIFICANT SENTENCE** among those said by Christopher Columbus (bolded in the text) and write it on the lines below.

_____

_____

_____

2. **PARAPHRASE** the sentence that you selected as being most significant.

_____

_____

_____

3. Ask a thought-provoking **QUESTION** to Christopher Columbus based on his own words from the ship's log.

_____

_____

_____

4. Identify what stood out to you as the main **PROBLEM** raised in this reading.

_____

_____

_____

5. If you were an Arawak Indian, what **QUESTION** would you ask Christopher Columbus about justice?

_____

_____

_____

6. What do you think Christopher Columbus's **CONCLUSION** was about the Arawak Indians?

_____

_____

_____

7. **SPEAKING IN THE AUTHOR'S VOICE**: Create a brief talk about "justice" between you and Christopher Columbus (C.C.) by filling in the dialogue lines that follow.

Note: This dialogue should be a thoughtful discussion of important ideas, not including lines such as "Hi, how are you?" "Thank you for your time," and so on.

You: _____

_____

C.C.: _____

_____

You: _____

_____

C.C.: _____

_____

You: _____

_____

C.C.: _____

_____

A Reading From *A People's History of the United States*

By Howard Zinn

Arawak men and women, naked, tawny, and full of wonder, emerged from their villages onto the island's beaches and swam out to get a closer look at the strange big boat. When Columbus and his sailors came ashore, carrying swords, speaking oddly, the Arawaks ran to greet them, brought them food, water, gifts. He later wrote of this in his log:

They ... brought us parrots and balls of cotton and spears and many other things, which they exchanged for the glass beads and hawks' bells. They willingly traded everything they owned. ... They were well-built, with good bodies and handsome features. ... They do not bear arms, and do not know them, for I showed them a sword, they took it by the edge and cut themselves out of ignorance. They have no iron. Their spears are made of cane. ... They would make fine servants. ... With fifty men we could subjugate them all and make them do whatever we want.

These Arawaks of the Bahama Islands were much like Indians on the mainland, who were remarkable (European observers were to say again and again) for their hospitality, their belief in sharing. These traits did not stand out in the Europe of the Renaissance, dominated as it was by the religion of popes, the government of kings, the frenzy for money that marked Western civilization and its first messenger to the Americas, Christopher Columbus.

Columbus wrote:

As soon as I arrived in the Indies, on the first Island which I found, I took some of the natives by force in order that they might learn and might give me information of whatever there is in these parts.

The information that Columbus wanted most was: Where is the gold? He had persuaded the king and queen of Spain to finance an expedition to the lands, the wealth, he expected would be on the other side of the Atlantic—the Indies and Asia, gold and spices. For, like other informed people of his time, he knew the world was round and he could sail west in order to get to the Far East.

Spain was recently unified, one of the new modern nation-states, like France, England, and Portugal. Its population, mostly poor peasants, worked for the nobility, who were 2 percent of the population and owned 95 percent of the land. Spain had tied itself to the Catholic Church, expelled all the Jews, driven out the Moors. Like other states of the modern world, Spain sought gold, which was becoming the new mark of wealth, more useful than land because it could buy anything.

There was gold in Asia, it was thought, and certainly silks and spices, for Marco Polo and others had brought back marvelous things from their overland expeditions centuries before. Now that the Turks had conquered Constantinople and the eastern Mediterranean, and controlled the land routes to Asia, a sea route was needed. Portuguese sailors were working their way around the southern tip of Africa. Spain decided to gamble on a long sail across an unknown ocean.

In return for bringing back gold and spices, they promised Columbus 10 percent of the profits, governorship over new-found lands, and the fame that would go with a new title: Admiral of the Ocean Sea. He was a merchant's clerk from the Italian city of Genoa, part-time weaver (the son of a skilled weaver), and expert sailor. He set out with three sailing ships, the largest of which was the *Santa Maria*, perhaps 100 feet long, and thirty-nine crew members.

Columbus would never have made it to Asia, which was thousands of miles farther away than he had calculated, imagining a smaller world. He would have been doomed by that great expanse of sea. But he was lucky. One-fourth of the way there he came upon an unknown, uncharted land that lay between Europe and Asia—the Americas. It was early October 1492, and thirty-three days since he and his crew had left the Canary Islands, off the Atlantic coast of Africa. Now they saw branches and sticks floating in the water. They saw flocks of birds.

These were signs of land. Then, on October 12, a sailor called Rodrigo saw the early morning moon shining on white sands, and cried out. It was an island in the Bahamas, the Caribbean Sea. The first man to sight land was supposed to get a yearly pension of 10,000 maravedis for life, but Rodrigo never got it. Columbus claimed he had seen a light the evening before. He got the reward.

So, approaching land, they were met by the Arawak Indians, who swam out to greet them. The Arawaks lived in village communes, had a developed agriculture of corn, yams, cassava. They could spin and weave, but they had no horses or work animals. They had no iron, but they wore tiny gold ornaments in their ears.

This was to have enormous consequences: it led Columbus to take some of them aboard ship as prisoners because he insisted that they guide him to the source of the gold. He then sailed to what is now Cuba, then to Hispaniola (the island which today consists of Haiti and the Dominican Republic). There, bits of visible gold in the rivers, and a gold mask presented to Columbus by a local Indian chief, led to wild visions of gold fields.

On Hispaniola, out of timbers from the *Santa Maria*, which had run aground, Columbus built a fort, the first European military base in the Western Hemisphere. He called it Navidad (Christmas) and left thirty-nine crewmembers there, with instructions to find and store the gold. He took more Indian prisoners and put them aboard his two remaining ships. At one part of the island he got into a fight with Indians who refused to trade as many bows and arrows as he and his men wanted. Two were run through with swords and bled to death. Then the *Nina* and the *Pinta* set sail for the Azores and Spain. When the weather turned cold, the Indian prisoners began to die.

Columbus's report to the Court in Madrid was extravagant. He insisted he had reached Asia (it was Cuba) and an island off the coast of China (Hispaniola). His descriptions were part fact, part fiction:

Hispaniola is a miracle. Mountains and hills, plains and pastures, are both fertile and beautiful ... the harbors are unbelievably good and there are many wide rivers of which the majority contain gold. ... There are many spices, and great mines of gold and other metals. ...

The Indians, Columbus reported, **"are so naive and so free with their possessions that no one who has not witnessed them would believe it. When you ask for something they have, they never say no. To the contrary, they offer to share with anyone ..."** He concluded his report by asking for a little help from their Majesties, and in return he would bring them from his next voyage **"as much gold as they need ... and as many slaves as they ask."** He was full of religious talk: **"Thus the eternal God, our Lord, gives victory to those who follow His way over apparent impossibilities."**

Source: Howard Zinn, "Columbus, The Indians, and Human Progress," *A People's History of the United States*, pp. 1-3. Copyright © 2005 by The Roam Agency. Reprinted with permission.

Figure 15.1: Source: Copyright © Badseed (CC BY-SA 2.0) at https://commons.wikimedia.org/wiki/File:Howard_Zinn_at_B-Fest_2009.jpg.

Closing Activity

Directions

- Respond to the three **prompts** that follow.

1. Create a **TITLE** for each of the following quotes and write them in the respective boxes.

> **Title:**

D arwin's theory of the struggle for existence and the selectivity connected with it has by many people been cited as authorization of the encouragement of the spirit of competition. Some people also in such a way have tried to prove pseudo-scientifically the necessity of the destructive economic struggle of competition between individuals. But this is wrong, because man owes his strength in the struggle for existence to the fact that he is a socially living animal. As little as a battle between ants of an ant hill is essential for survival, just so little is this the case with the individual members of a human community.

"Therefore, one should guard against preaching to the young man success in the customary sense as the aim of life. For a successful man is he who receives a great deal from his fellowmen, usually incomparably more than corresponds to his service to them. The value of a man, however, should be seen in what he gives and not in what he is able to receive."

—Albert Einstein

Source: Albert Einstein, *Out of My Later Years*, pp. 37. Copyright © 1950 by Kensington Publishing Corp. Reprinted with permission.

Figure 15.2: Source: http://commons.wikimedia.org/wiki/File:Einstein1921_by_F_Schmutzer_2.jpg.

The highest test of the civilization of any race is in its willingness to lend a helping hand to the less fortunate. A race, like an individual, lifts itself up by lifting others up. It requires little wisdom or statesmanship to crush out the aspirations of a people, but the highest and most profound statesmanship is shown in guiding and stimulating a people."

—*Booker T. Washington*

2. What do you think was Albert Einstein's and Booker T. Washington's PURPOSE in writing these words?

3. What do you think will be one CONSEQUENCE for the future of humanity if we fail to understand and follow these words by Albert Einstein and Booker T. Washington?

Figure 15.3: Source: http://commons.wikimedia.org/wiki/File:Booker_T._Washington.JPG.

Homework

Directions

- Write an opinion paper about the problem Howard Zinn raised in his book excerpt about Christopher Columbus that particularly caught your attention.

- You responded to several **prompts** today. Use these thoughts to guide you as you write. *Note: Include the **QUOTE** you cited for the **SPEAK IN THE AUTHOR'S VOICE** tool.*

Reflection on Book Excerpt
"Happiness" by Swami Ramananda

OA Quote, Mahatma Gandhi

MA Book Excerpt, Swami Ramananda

CA Philosophy Textbook Excerpt, Socrates

HW Book Excerpt, Swami Ramananda

"What is worth learning is worth learning well."

—Alfred North Whitehead

Opening Activity

Directions

- **PARAPHRASE** the following quote.
- Respond to the prompt that follows.
- Complete the peer review.

"Be the change you want to see in the world."

—Mahatma Gandhi

_____

_____

_____

If you try to act on these words of Mahatma Gandhi, what do you think will be one important **CONSEQUENCE** for how you live each day?

_____

_____

_____

Figure 16.1: Source: http://commons.wikimedia.org/wiki/File:Mohandas_K._Gandhi,_portrait.jpg.

Main Activity

Directions

- Read the chapter from the book by Swami Ramananda that appears on the following pages.

- Respond to the following **prompts** that follow in clear, complete sentences.

1. What was the author's **PURPOSE** in writing this excerpt?

_____

_____

_____

2. Select and underline in the text what you think is the most **SIGNIFICANT SENTENCE** and explain why you selected it.

_____

_____

_____

3. What **QUESTION** about happiness is raised for you after reading this excerpt?

_____

_____

_____

4. What is one **CONSEQUENCE** for our lives if we follow what the author recommends in the reading?

_____

_____

_____

5. Use the responses you gave in **prompts** #1–4 (and other thoughts you may have) to describe how this reading affected what you consider to be your goals in life. Write one short paragraph.

_____

_____

_____

_____

_____

_____

_____

_____

Happiness

By Swami Ramananda

The moneyed ones are not all happy, nor are the poor. The middle class people cannot claim happiness either as their exclusive possessions. Men of the same economic status are not equally happy. And, there are families drawing a bare maintenance which are happy and contented. So, what does happiness depend upon? Does it depend upon what we possess, or get from outside? Man today believes that it does. The conviction has unconsciously gone deep down into his being, or else he should not be mad after the good things of the world as he is today.

This is the greatest delusion of the age; happiness varies directly as the material gains. If one hundred rupees would buy one unit of happiness, two hundred would buy just the double. Power is believed to vary as possessions. Therefore, happiness varies as power, varies as possessions. This has maddened man. The all out war for possessions has made him inhuman. He destroys the very happiness for which he fights. It is mockery of human intelligence.

Happiness does not depend upon gains, nor does it depend upon their absence. It does not depend upon the respect that we have from others, nor upon its opposite. Look around with an open eye and you will discover the truth of this fact. Happiness depends neither upon smooth sailing in life, nor on the reverse.

In a way it does depend upon all these, because it depends upon how we react to our circumstances. It depends upon how we accept the situations of life and what we are ready to give to others. Proper acceptance means correct adjustment and that is the secret of happiness. Then we are able to give to others the best that we can. This enhances our happiness and accelerates our growth.

A man may sit and weep over the loss of his money. Another may refuse to worry over it. 'What is gone is gone. Look ahead.' He may think. He may soon make more than he has lost and gain a position which he had never thought of. The other man who worries may lose heart and become an invalid for life! Not only the loss of money, I have seen people accepting failures and still more serious things cheerfully. Even the death of dear and near ones can be accepted properly. Misery does not lie in the outward event. If it did, all should be equally miserable in the face of similar circumstances. But, they are not. Misery or happiness lies in our attitudes, the way we accept things.

This is the great lesson that you have to learn. Cease to blame the world. Cease to blame your destiny for your unhappiness. You can be happy where you stand. Only look out properly. If you refuse to learn none can make you happy. Even the best of circumstances cannot make you happy. Your misery is self-created. Change your attitude towards life.

Can you believe in evolution? Do you believe in the existence of the Lord? Do you believe in the Master of Evolution, the Divine Mother? If you really do, and understand what it means, how can you be unhappy? You cannot but accept every circumstance as Divine dispensation and for your good. You have got to make the best of everything. Life will become to you a series of joys, a perpetual flow of Her grace, if you can do so.

'It is sheer idealism' you will say. It is idealism, no doubt, for it demands of you to lift your eyes up. But, it is practical idealism. It is an idealism based on the truth of things. It is perfectly practicable. Try it, but patiently.

'There are physical pains,' you would say. Yes. 'They are torturing,' no doubt. But they have their meaning, message and utility. They are not in vain. You cannot escape them. Why not accept them as best as you can.

The better the acceptance of circumstances the more can you give to others. It is your Karma of the past, that is fruitening in the form of circumstances of your present. You are reaping what you sowed in the past. It has no direct importance from the point of view of evolution. It is like a spent up bullet. Of real importance is what you can give to others. That is what fashions you. That is effective in your evolution. If you cannot give love and are giving hatred, you are injuring yourself. You are darkening your future. You are not aiding in your evolution. Cynicism is suicidal.

If you are not able to serve others cheerfully, if you resist opportunities of service, it is bad. You are throwing away chances to grow.

Love, service and sacrifice are precious opportunities for aspirants. Only unfortunate ones reject them. The more you can give, the happier will you be in life.

But, happiness you must know is not the goal of life. Proper adjustment is necessary. It automatically results from right understanding of life. It is essential for further growth. Right adjustment is simply the art of right living. Life is given us for the unfoldment of the higher principles of Wisdom and Love, for the perfect unfoldment of Divinity. Happiness is by far transcended in Bliss.

Joy is the thrill of the moment. Happiness is the general state of rhythmic balance in our inner consciousness. Desire underlies momentary thrills. Desire, effort and fulfilment are the three spokes of the wheel of joy. One fulfilment gives birth to another desire and the wheel revolves on. It moves on rotating around its axle, the ego. Man is never satiated. It is childish to be seeking momentary thrills. Life has a better use.

Proper adjustment is the greatest problem of life. It depends upon our understanding of life, our acceptance and our reaction to it. That determines our happiness or misery. We by ourselves happy or miserable, but foolishly blame the world. Shoulder this responsibility. If you shoulder it, then alone can you remold yourself and make yourself happy. If you do not, who can help you? This sense of responsibility is the prior condition for any self-effort to aid yourself. You must know the art of living, before you can accelerate your evolution.

Right understanding and right living are the first two basic lessons of spiritual practice. Do not minimize their importance. Know the truth and live in accordance with it. Truth alone can deliver the goods.

Closing Activity

Directions

- Read the philosophy textbook excerpt that appears on the following pages.
- Respond to the **prompts** that follow in clear and complete sentences.

1. What was the author's **PURPOSE** in writing this philosophy textbook excerpt?

_____

_____

_____

2. Underline in the text what you think is the most **SIGNIFICANT SENTENCE** in this excerpt and then explain why you selected this sentence.

_____

_____

_____

3. What **QUESTION** is raised for you after having read this excerpt?

_____

_____

_____

4. Use the responses you gave on the previous page (and other thoughts you have) to describe in one short paragraph how you can use Socrates's idea of "questioning" and the "use of reason" to get to the truth.

_____

_____

_____

_____

_____

_____

_____

_____

Socrates the Philosopher

By Alan Haworth

The fact that Socrates never put his thoughts down in writing distinguishes him from every later philosopher. Whereas the others are remembered mainly through their books, Socrates practiced philosophy by means of a purely 'word of mouth' technique. To the Athenians he was a familiar figure. They would encounter him in the marketplace as he debated philosophical questions with anyone prepared to engage in a discussion with him. This can make Socrates appear truly remarkable to present day philosophers.

However, it doesn't really make him as remarkable as all that, for Socrates was a contemporary of the *sophists*, wandering scholars who would, in the typical case, move from place to place, providing tuition in return for a fee. There were many sophists and, like Socrates, all tended to work through speech rather than writing. So, it wasn't the simple fact that Socrates practiced his teaching orally, in public, which made him so exceptional. If we are to understand what it was, we must consider how Socrates and the sophists differed.

There were a number of differences. One was that, unlike most sophists, Socrates made no charge for his services. Another was that, whereas most sophists travelled from place to place in the course of their work, Socrates left Athens only once in his life. More significantly from our point of view, Socrates and the sophists differed in the reasons they had for working as they did. On the one hand, it was Socrates' opinion that philosophy could only be properly taught and practiced orally. 'Dialectic' was the route to truth. As this suggests, it would be wrong to think that Socrates just never found the time to write, or—perhaps—that he never managed to make the effort. On the contrary, he considered writing an inappropriate technique. (I think most present day philosophers would agree with him that discussion is central to philosophy, although they would be less dismissive of the written text.) It is consistent with this interest in truth that Socrates should have insisted, as he did, on the primacy of reason and logic, on *rationality*. His approach would be to challenge the person with whom he was arguing to formulate a definition of the thing—usually a virtue—they were discussing. Socrates would then call the definition into question, forcing his opponent to defend it. (This has come to be known as 'the Socratic method'.)

By contrast with Socrates, the sophists tended to attach more importance to the arts of rhetoric and persuasion than they ever did to seeking truth through the use of reason. The opinion of one sophist—a contemporary of Plato's called Isocrates—is on record. According to him, 'likely conjecture about useful things is far preferable to exact knowledge of the useless' (Isocrates 1954–6: 63). Socrates strongly disapproved.

In fact, it is easy to appreciate why the sophists took this attitude in favour of rhetoric. It is what they were hired to teach. There was a demand for their services, partly because anyone who lacked the skill of speaking persuasively in public could never succeed in getting his[3] way at meetings of the Assembly, Athens' supreme legislative institution. The Assembly passed laws, and decisions of policy were made there. It met every ten days or so, and any citizen could attend and speak. When you think that citizens composed roughly a quarter of the population, you can imagine how large the more well-attended meetings must have been. (There were about 30,000 citizens in all and, out of that number, about 6,000 regularly attended meetings of the assembly.) Moreover, if a citizen took out a case against you, the legal system required that you should be tried before a court of fellow citizens, usually numbered in hundreds. You would have to defend yourself. No wonder it was so important to the Athenian citizen that he should master the skill of persuading others by rhetoric, and that sophists were able to command high fees for teaching it. Some sophists may also have been experts in this or that field of learning but, if they taught that too, it came secondarily, as a bonus.

To sum up, then, one difference between the typical sophist and Socrates was this. Whereas the sophist taught rhetoric and sometimes claimed specialist knowledge, Socrates sought truth through the use of reason. More than that, far from claiming to know anything, Socrates professed ignorance. At his trial, in his address to the jury, Socrates related a story about it. He claimed that an old friend of his, Chaerophon, once visited the oracle at Delphi and asked the god whether there was anyone wiser than Socrates himself. Apparently, the god replied that there was not. According to the story, when he heard of this Socrates was so puzzled that he set about interviewing those with a reputation for wisdom. It turned out that no one's pretensions to knowledge could survive Socratic interrogation. Therefore—and here is the moral—only Socrates knew that he knew nothing, and it was this knowledge which made him wiser than everyone else (Plato 1954a: 49ff).

Source: Alan Haworth, "Socrates (The Philosopher)," *Understanding the Political Philosophers: From Ancient to Modern Times*, pp. 8-9. Copyright © 2004 by Taylor & Francis Group. Reprinted with permission.

Homework

Directions

- Read the chapter from the book by Swami Ramananda that appears on the following pages.
- Respond to the **prompts** that follow in clear, complete sentences.

1. What do you think was Swami Ramananda's **PURPOSE** in writing this chapter?

_____

_____

_____

2. Underline in the text what you think is the most **SIGNIFICANT SENTENCE** in this excerpt. Explain why you selected it.

_____

_____

_____

PARAPHRASE the sentence you selected earlier as being most significant.

_____

_____

_____

3. Think of one **CONSEQUENCE** that would result if we look at our fellow human beings as Swami Ramananda suggests we do.

_____

_____

_____

4. In light of this chapter, how would you **RECOMMEND** we better understand the experiences that come to us in life?

_____

_____

_____

Spiritualism

By Swami Ramananda

Spiritualism is like a [1]bug-bear to those who do not understand it. As I understand it, it is not a rejection of life. Nor is it a massacre of one's susceptibilities. It is, rather, the total acceptance of life, with all its shortcomings. It is an integral outlook on life. It leaves out no side of it. It aspires to a fullness of life, to a holiness which is wholeness. Those who have formed an erroneous idea of spiritualism alone fight shy of it.

People make water-tight compartments: spiritual and material. It is meaningless. The Divine embraces all. Nothing is outside the ken of the Master of Evolution. The evolutionary process embraces all alike. The man who is leading a fast life is also undergoing the process of evolution, as the one who is given to meditation and prayer. One who is grovelling in filth is on the same ladder as the one who is clean. Only, they are at different rungs. This is all spiritual evolution. All experience is spiritual. All endeavour is spiritual. It is contributing to the one single process which is going on variously in the universe.

Spiritualism is an endeavour to trace the Divine thread through one and all alike. It is an attempt to recognize Him at work everywhere from the stirrings in a living cell to human beings, from a speck of dust to a mountain, from the humble hearth of a peasant to the palace of a king. It is to catch the glimmer of His light in the materialist and the spiritualist, in the sinner and the saint, in the ant and the elephant alike. It comprises an infinite breadth of vision, a giddy height of comprehension and embraces all at a glance.

The spiritual man can exclude none. He can hate none. He has to accept all. He has to embrace all. The Divine dwells in all alike. Whom can he reject?

Spiritualism is such an outlook. It does not incapacitate man for action. It teaches that action is the path of spiritual growth. Duty is sacred according to it. It is the line of one's evolution. It is worship, for the Master of Evolution accepts the offerings of work. Work in proper spirit lifts as nothing else.

---

1   **bug-bear, noun:** *a cause of anxiety or irritation*

Experience is indispensable for evolution. So there arises no question of shunning life. Seclusion is a temporary measure, needed to equip oneself to be able to better share in the Divine Sacrifice, the world-play. It is no ideal. It is not to be aspired for. It has no value in itself.

Spiritualism teaches no escape from life. It advocates no cowardice. It does just the reverse. Problems are inevitable in life. Sufferings and failures are quite natural. They have to be accepted, but not merely because they are inevitable. They have to be accepted cheerfully. They are the harbingers of rapid growth.

Spiritualism does not mean an apathy towards the world. It means self-less love, sympathy and service. It means an utter negation of selfishness. The world in which spiritualism dominates will become filled with joy. It will become a happy place to live in, where human beings do not fly at one another's throat. They love, live and let live. They are human, worthy to be called men, sons of God.

Spiritualism raises a vision of the Divine Life before man. It calls him to fulfill his noble destiny. It studies the higher aspects of evolution i.e., superhuman stage, and shows the way to it.

Transcend desire. Transcend greed and passion. Transcend hatred and malice. Transcend attachment. Transcend all that is lower, all that is for misery and keeps man down. Transcend it all. Do not kill it. It has all to be transcended in due course. Its transcendence is inevitable. You may hasten it by proper effort, and can sooner pass into Divinity. You may aid your younger brethren to pass on quicker to their fulfilment by doing so yourself.

Spiritualism advocates no suppression, nor does it advocate indulgence. Understand. Change the structure of your whole being so that indulgence can no longer fit in. Transform your entire constitution by outgrowing your present stage so that the energy of sex becomes the light of pure love. Thus there remains no question of suppressions.

Life is the road to Divinity. As you move ahead all these lower tendencies will be left behind. The faster you move the quicker you will leave them behind.

Spiritualism talks not of sin. It accepts the necessity of erring for growth and gives man the freedom to do so. We have to pay for all that we do. That is good. It is educative. It aids the process of evolution. Spiritualism talks not of prohibitions, but awakens man to an understanding of the plan that is evolution. It shows him what is what in evolution. It gives him a sense of values. It threatens not. It frightens not man with eternal damnation. Freedom is essential for growth. It respects human freedom to err.

It advocates the higher life, but accepts you where you stand. It is not impatient. It knows of infinite future life wherein growth is possible. It has an ever-fresh message of hope. It knows of no failure, and of no frustration. It knows of marching on and on. It knows only success. There can be no failure. From joy to greater joy it leads.

You will find a stay in spiritualism when all the stays of life are gone. You will find light when all the lights have failed you. You will discover an order where apparently there ranks chaos. In utter despair you will find hope. Spiritualism will come as a mother when out of bewilderment, you are ready to cut your throat. It will show that life has a meaning and a purpose. It will tell you that even the most unworthy in the world is worthy enough to live and love. It can bring hope to the frustrated and life to the almost dead.

Suicides are on the increase. Why? Man does not know the value of life. The value he foolishly attaches to it is so small that it is no value. Life is a twopence which can be done away with in a trice. This is the result of our philosophy of life.

To make material ends the highest in life is to invite doom. It is to play in the hands of the lower nature. It is to fall a willing victim to that demoness, desire. She captivates. She kindles a fire which consumes all. Material ends cannot satiate. Desire grows; man envies man. He is jealous. He grows inimical, and fights. He is frustrated. Life becomes meaningless and he quickly does away with it. "If pleasure is the object of living what use is it living when there is no pleasure?" This is perfect logic. Man should be justified to kill himself. I wonder why man is called to account for attempting to do so. Man, according to this philosophy, should have the right to kill himself: consistency demands it. In the race for the good things of the world, all cannot come out first. But, none is prepared to stand second!

The materialistic outlook on life advocates material ends as the highest: there is nothing higher and nobler than material joys. Where does it lead to? To the war theatre, to the concentration-camp, and to the self-fitted beloved gallows! It leads to the pistol-bullet which can so readily despatch. It creates war of nerves. It creates heats and panics. It makes man out and out a beast. That outlook is a delusion. It is a self-contradiction. It is based on ignorance of the real nature of pleasure. It betrays the shortness of vision. The last century has demonstrated the hollowness of it.

It can give no real morality. All that it can advocate is a police-man morality. It is not bad to thieve, but it is certainly bad to be caught, declared and punished. Evil is evil, not because of itself, but because it brings punishment. This exposes the bankruptcy of this outlook.

This materialistic outlook on life has also got a place in the evolutionary course of things. When the reasoning mind evolves, the desire-principle is stimulated, and it in its turn stimulates the lower nature, and the reasoning mind, along with the ego. Nothing better than such a limited vision is possible. Humanity at large is passing through this stage of evolution at present, and it is no wonder that it is suffering as it does.

The inherent self-contradiction of materialism i.e. the very pursuit of material ends destroys them, prepares the field for the advent of the higher principle, Wisdom. The self-inflicted civilized torture of man is driving him on. Mankind is in travail.

Spiritualism advocates no escape from activity. It is not action which binds, but desire. Money does not bind: it is greed that does so. Woman does not drag, but it is lust that does. It advocates a higher and constructive outlook on life. It does not reject pleasures, but it does teach that they are no ends in themselves. Human life has a higher purpose.

Humanity today is passing through a critical stage. Man's suffering has reached a climax. His lower nature is like an active volcano which is raining liquid fire and stone. Man is calling for help, but in vain. Help is to come from within, not without. The dawn of Wisdom can alone solve the problem of humanity. Spiritualism denotes this dawn, but it can be appreciated only when mankind is ready for the coming step, not till then.

Name: _____

Date: _____

Analysis of History Textbook Excerpt *A People's History of the United States*

OA   Quote, Abraham Lincoln

MA   Book Excerpt, Howard Zinn

CA   Letter, Dr. Martin Luther King Jr.

HW   Letter, Dr. Martin Luther King Jr.

"What is worth learning is worth learning well."

—Alfred North Whitehead

Opening Activity

Directions

- **PARAPHRASE** the following quote in one or two clear and complete sentences.

Figure 17.1: Source: http://pixabay.com/en/president-abraham-lincoln-man-391128/.

"It has been said of the world's history that 'might makes right.' It is for us and for our times to reverse the maxim and to show that 'right makes might.'"

—Abraham Lincoln

_____

_____

_____

Main Activity

Directions

- Read the history textbook excerpt that appears after the four prompts.
- Respond to the **prompts** that follow in clear and complete sentences.

1. Create a **TITLE** for this textbook excerpt.

_____

2. Underline in the text the sentence that you think is most **SIGNIFICANT** in this excerpt. Explain why you selected this as the most significant sentence.

_____

_____

_____

_____

3. What **QUESTION** does this reading raise for you?

_____

_____

_____

4. Expand upon the responses you gave earlier to write a brief letter to President Johnson about the problem described in the excerpt.

_____

_____

_____

A Reading From *A People's History of the United States*

By Howard Zinn

In Albany, Georgia, a small deep-South town where the atmosphere of slavery still lingered, mass demonstrations took place in the winter of 1961 and again in 1962. Of 22,000 black people in Albany, over a thousand went to jail for marching, assembling, to protest segregation and discrimination. Here, as in all the demonstrations that would sweep over the South, little black children participated—a new generation was learning to act. The Albany police chief, after one of the mass arrests, was taking the names of prisoners lined up before his desk. He looked up and saw a Negro boy about nine years old. "What's your name?" The boy looked straight at him and said: "Freedom, Freedom."

There is no way of measuring the effect of that southern movement on the sensibilities of a whole generation of young black people, or of tracing the process by which some of them became activists and leaders. In Lee County, Georgia, after the events of 1961–1962, a black teenager named James Crawford joined SNCC and began taking black people to the county courthouse to vote. One day, bringing a woman there, he was approached by the deputy registrar. Another SNCC worker took notes on the conversation:

REGISTRAR: What do you want?

CRAWFORD: I brought this lady down to register.

REGISTRAR: (after giving the woman a card to fill out and sending her outside in the hall) Why did you bring this lady down here?

CRAWFORD: Because she wants to be a first class citizen like y'all.

REGISTRAR: Who are you to bring people down to register?

CRAWFORD: It's my job.

REGISTRAR: Suppose you get two bullets in your head right now?

CRAWFORD: I got to die anyhow.

REGISTRAR: If I don't do it, I can get somebody else to do it. (No reply.)

REGISTRAR: Are you scared?

CRAWFORD: No.

REGISTRAR: Suppose somebody came in that door and shoot you in the back of the head right now. What would you do?

CRAWFORD: I couldn't do nothing. If they shoot me in the back of the head there are people coming from all over the world.

REGISTRAR: What people?

CRAWFORD: The people I work for.

In Birmingham in 1963, thousands of blacks went into the streets, facing police clubs, tear gas, dogs, high-powered water hoses. And meanwhile, all over the deep South, the young people of SNCC, mostly black, a few white, were moving into communities in Georgia, Alabama, Mississippi, Arkansas. Joined by local black people, they were organizing, to register people to vote, to protest against racism, to build up courage against violence. The Department of Justice recorded 1412 demonstrations in three months of 1963. Imprisonment became commonplace, beatings became frequent. Many local people were afraid. Others came forward. A nineteen-year-old black student from Illinois named Carver Neblett, working for SNCC in Terrell County, Georgia, reported:

I talked with a blind man who is extremely interested in the civil rights movement. He has been keeping up with the movement from the beginning. Even though this man is blind he wants to learn all the questions on the literacy test. Imagine, while many are afraid that white men will burn our houses, shoot into them, or put us off their property, a blind man, seventy years old, wants to come to our meetings.

As the summer of 1964 approached, SNCC and other civil rights groups working together in Mississippi, and facing increasing violence, decided to call upon young people from other parts of the country for help. They hoped that would bring attention to the situation in Mississippi. Again and again in Mississippi and elsewhere, the FBI had stood by, lawyers for the Justice Department had stood by, while civil rights workers were beaten and jailed, while federal laws were violated.

On the eve of the Mississippi Summer, in early June 1964, the civil rights movement rented a theater near the White House, and a busload of black Mississippians traveled to Washington to testify publicly about the daily violence, the dangers facing the volunteers coming into Mississippi. Constitutional lawyers testified that the national government had the legal power to give protection against such violence. The transcript of this testimony was given to President Johnson and Attorney General Kennedy, accompanied by a request for a protective federal presence during the Mississippi Summer. There was no response.

Twelve days after the public hearing, three civil rights workers, James Chaney, a young black Mississippian, and two white volunteers, Andrew Goodman and Michael Schwerner, were arrested in Philadelphia, Mississippi, released from jail late at night, then seized, beaten with chains, and shot to death. Ultimately, an informer's testimony led to jail sentences for the sheriff and deputy sheriff and others. That came too late. The Mississippi murders had taken place after the repeated refusal of the national government, under Kennedy or Johnson, or any other President, to defend blacks against violence.

Source: Howard Zinn, *A People's History of the United States,* pp. 446-448. Copyright © 2005 by The Roam Agency. Reprinted with permission.

Closing Activity

Directions

- Read the letter by Dr. Martin Luther King Jr. that appears in the following pages.
- Respond to the **prompts** that follow in clear, complete sentences.

1. What do you think Dr. Martin Luther King Jr.'s **PURPOSE** was in writing this letter?

_____

_____

_____

2. Select and <u>underline</u> in the text what you think is the most **SIGNIFICANT SENTENCE**. Explain **why** you selected this as the most significant sentence.

_____

_____

_____

3. What is one **ASSUMPTION** Dr. Martin Luther King Jr. makes about "injustice" in this letter?

_____

_____

_____

4. If Dr. Martin Luther King Jr. were with you right now, what **QUESTION** would you like to ask him about this letter, which he wrote from the Birmingham city jail?

_____

_____

_____

5. You are an editor of a newspaper, and you are about to print this letter by Dr. Martin Luther King Jr. Create a **TITLE** for this letter and write it in the box on the following page.

_____

Martin Luther King, Jr.
Birmingham City Jail
April 16, 1963

My dear Fellow Clergymen,

While confined here in the Birmingham City Jail, I came across your recent statement calling our present activities "unwise and untimely." Seldom, if ever, do I pause to answer criticism of my work and ideas. If I sought to answer all the criticisms that cross my desk, my secretaries would be engaged in little else in the course of the day and I would have no time for constructive work. But since I feel that you are men of genuine goodwill and your criticisms are sincerely set forth, I would like to answer your statement in what I hope will be patient and reasonable terms.

I think I should give the reason for my being in Birmingham, since you have been influenced by the argument of "outsiders coming in." I have the honor of serving as president of the Southern Christian Leadership Conference, an organization operating in every Southern state with headquarters in Atlanta, Georgia. We have some eighty-five affiliate organizations all across the South—one being the Alabama Christian Movement for Human Rights. Whenever necessary and possible we share staff, educational, and financial resources with our affiliates. Several months ago our local affiliate here in Birmingham invited us to be on call to engage in a nonviolent direct action program if such were deemed necessary. We readily consented and when the hour came we lived up to our promises. So I am here, along with several members of my staff, because we were invited here. I am here because I have basic organizational ties here. Beyond this, I am in Birmingham because injustice is here. Just as the eighth century prophets left their little villages and carried their "thus saith the Lord" far beyond the boundaries of their home town, and just as the Apostle Paul left his little village of Tarsus and carried the gospel of Jesus Christ to practically every hamlet and city of the Graeco-Roman world, I too am compelled to carry the gospel of freedom beyond my particular home town. Like Paul, I must constantly respond to the Macedonian call for aid.

Moreover, I am cognizant of the interrelatedness of all communities and states. I cannot sit idly by in Atlanta and not be concerned about what happens in Birmingham. Injustice anywhere is a threat to justice everywhere. We are caught in an inescapable network of mutuality tied in a single garment of destiny. Whatever affects one directly affects all indirectly. Never again can we afford to live with the narrow, provincial "outside agitator" idea. Anyone who lives inside the United States can never be considered an outsider anywhere in this country.

You deplore the demonstrations that are presently taking place in Birmingham. But I am sorry that your statement did not express a similar concern for the conditions that brought the demonstrations into being. I am sure that each of you would want to go beyond the superficial social analyst who looks merely at effects, and does not grapple with underlying causes. I would not hesitate to say that it is unfortunate that so-called demonstrations are taking place in Birmingham at this time, but I would say in more emphatic terms that it is even more unfortunate that the white power structure of this city left the Negro community with no other alternative.

In any nonviolent campaign there are four basic steps: (1) Collection of the facts to determine whether injustices are alive; (2) Negotiation; (3) Self-purification; and (4) Direct action. We have gone through all of these steps in Birmingham. There can be no gainsaying of the fact that racial injustice engulfs this community. Birmingham is probably the most thoroughly segregated city in the United States. Its ugly record of police brutality is known in every section of this country. Its unjust treatment of Negroes in the courts is a notorious reality. There have been more unsolved bombings of Negro homes and churches in Birmingham than any city in this nation. These are the hard, brutal, and unbelievable facts. On the basis of these conditions Negro leaders sought to negotiate with the city fathers. But the political leaders consistently refused to engage in good faith negotiation.

Then came the opportunity last September to talk with some of the leaders of the economic community. In these negotiating sessions certain promises were made by the merchants—such as the promise to remove the humiliating racial signs from the stores. On the basis of these promises Rev. Shuttlesworth and the leaders of the Alabama Christian Movement for Human Rights agreed to call a moratorium on any type of demonstrations. As the weeks and months unfolded we realized that we were the victims of a broken promise. The signs remained. As in so many experiences of the past we were confronted with blasted hopes, and the dark shadow of a deep disappointment settled upon us. So we had no alternative except that of preparing for direct action, whereby we would present our very bodies as a means of laying our case before the conscience of the local and national community. We were not unmindful of the difficulties involved. So we decided to go through a process of self-purification. We started having workshops on nonviolence and repeatedly asked ourselves the questions, "Are you able to accept blows without retaliating?" "Are you able to endure the ordeals of jail?"

We decided to set our direct-action program around the Easter season, realizing that with the exception of Christmas, this was the largest shopping period of the year. Knowing that a strong economic withdrawal program would be the by-product of direct action, we felt that this was the best time to bring pressure on the merchants for the needed changes. Then it occurred to us that the March election was ahead, and so we speedily decided to postpone action until after election day. When we discovered that Mr. Connor was in the run-off, we decided again to postpone action so that the demonstrations could not be used to cloud the issues. At this time we agreed to begin our nonviolent witness the day after the run-off.

This reveals that we did not move irresponsibly into direct action. We too wanted to see Mr. Connor defeated; so we went through postponement after postponement to aid in this community need. After this we felt that direct action could be delayed no longer.

You may well ask, Why direct action? Why sit-ins, marches, etc.? Isn't negotiation a better path?" You are exactly right in your call for negotiation. Indeed, this is the purpose of direct action. Nonviolent direct action seeks to create such a crisis and establish such creative tension that a community that has constantly refused to negotiate is forced to confront the issue. It seeks so to dramatize the issue that it can no longer be ignored. I just referred to the creation of tension as a part of the work of the nonviolent resister. This may sound rather shocking. But I must confess that I am not afraid of the word tension. I have earnestly worked and preached against violent tension, but there is a type of constructive nonviolent tension that is necessary for growth. Just as Socrates felt that it was necessary to create a tension in the mind so that individuals could rise from the bondage of myths and half-truths to the unfettered realm of creative analysis and objective appraisal, we must see the need of having nonviolent gadflies to create the kind of tension in society that will help men rise from the dark depths of prejudice and racism to the majestic heights of understanding and brotherhood. So the purpose of the direct action is to create a situation so crisis-packed that it will inevitably open the door to negotiation. We, therefore, concur with you in your call for negotiation. Too long has our beloved Southland been bogged down in the tragic attempt to live in monologue rather than dialogue.

One of the basic points in your statement is that our acts are untimely. Some have asked, "Why didn't you give the new administration time to act?" The only answer that I can give to this inquiry is that the new administration must be prodded about as much as the outgoing one before it acts. We will be sadly mistaken if we feel that the election of Mr. Boutwell will bring the millennium to Birmingham. While Mr. Boutwell is much more articulate and gentle than Mr. Connor, they are both segregationists dedicated to the task of maintaining the status quo. The hope I see in Mr. Boutwell is that he will be reasonable enough to see the futility of massive resistance to desegregation. But he will not see this without pressure from the devotees of civil rights. My friends, I must say to you that we have not made a single gain in civil rights without determined legal and nonviolent pressure. History is the long and tragic story of the fact that privileged groups seldom give up their privileges voluntarily. Individuals may see the moral light and voluntarily give up their unjust posture; but as Reinhold Niebuhr has reminded us, groups are more immoral than individuals.

We know through painful experience that freedom is never voluntarily given by the oppressor; it must be demanded by the oppressed. Frankly I have never yet engaged in a direct action movement that was "well timed," according to the timetable of those who have not suffered unduly from the disease of segregation. For years now I have heard the word "Wait!" It rings in the ear of every Negro with a piercing familiarity. This "wait" has almost always meant "never." It has been a tranquilizing thalidomide, relieving the emotional stress for a moment, only to give birth to an ill-formed infant of frustration. We must come to see with the distinguished jurist of yesterday that "justice too long delayed is justice denied." We have waited for more than three hundred and forty years for our constitutional and God-given rights. The nations of Asia and Africa are moving with jet-like speed toward the goal of political independence, and we still creep at horse and buggy pace toward the gaining of a cup of coffee at a lunch counter.

I guess it is easy for those who have never felt the stinging darts of segregation to say wait. But when you have seen vicious mobs lynch your mothers and fathers at will and drown your sisters and brothers at whim; when you have seen hate filled policemen curse, kick, brutalize, and even kill your black brothers and sisters with impunity; when you see the vast majority of your twenty million Negro brothers smothering in an air-tight cage of poverty in the midst of an affluent society; when you suddenly find your tongue twisted and your speech stammering as you seek to explain to your six-year-old daughter why she can't go to the public amusement park that has just been advertised on television, and see tears welling up in her little eyes when she is told that Funtown is closed to colored children, and see the depressing clouds of inferiority begin to form in her little mental sky, and see her begin to distort her little personality by unconsciously developing a bitterness toward white people; when you have to concoct an answer for a five-year-old son asking in agonizing pathos: "Daddy, why do white people treat colored people so mean?"; when you take a cross-country drive and find it necessary to sleep night after night in the uncomfortable corners of your automobile because no motel will accept you; when you are humiliated day in and day out by nagging signs reading "white" men and "colored"; when your first name becomes "nigger" and your middle name becomes "boy" (however old you are) and your last name becomes "John," and when your wife and mother are never given the respected title "Mrs."; when you are harried by day and haunted by night by the fact that you are a Negro, living constantly at tip-toe stance never quite knowing what to expect next, and plagued with inner fears and outer resentments; when you are forever fighting a degenerating sense of "nobodiness"—then you will understand why we find it difficult to wait.

There comes a time when the cup of endurance runs over, and men are no longer willing to be plunged into an abyss of injustice where they experience the bleakness of corroding despair. I hope, sirs, you can understand our legitimate and unavoidable impatience.

You express a great deal of anxiety over our willingness to break laws. This is certainly a legitimate concern. Since we so diligently urge people to obey the Supreme Court's decision of 1954 outlawing segregation in the public schools, it is rather strange and paradoxical to find us consciously breaking laws. One may well ask: "How can you advocate breaking some laws and obeying others?" The answer is found in the fact that there are two types of laws: There are just laws and there are unjust laws. I would be the first to advocate obeying just laws. One has not only a legal but moral responsibility to obey just laws. Conversely, one has a moral responsibility to disobey unjust laws. I would agree with Saint Augustine that "An unjust law is no law at all."

Now what is the difference between the two? How does one determine when a law is just or unjust? A just law is a man-made code that squares with the moral law or the law of God. An unjust law is a code that is out of harmony with the moral law. To put it in the terms of Saint Thomas Aquinas, an unjust law is a human law that is not rooted in eternal and natural law. Any law that uplifts human personality is just. Any law that degrades human personality is unjust. All segregation statutes are unjust because segregation distorts the soul and damages the personality. It gives the segregator a false sense of superiority and the segregated a false sense of inferiority. To use the words of Martin Buber, the great Jewish philosopher, segregation substitutes an "I-it" relationship for an "I-thou" relationship, and ends up relegating persons to the status of things. So segregation is not only politically, economically, and sociologically unsound, but it is morally wrong and sinful. Paul Tillich has said that sin is separation. Isn't segregation an existential expression of man's tragic separation, an expression of his awful estrangement, his terrible sinfulness? So I can urge men to obey the 1954 decision of the Supreme Court because it is morally right, and I can urge them to disobey segregation ordinances because they are morally wrong. [...].

Yours for the cause of
Peace and Brotherhood,

Martin Luther King, Jr.

Source: Martin Luther King, Jr, "Letter from a Birmingham Jail," 1963.

Figure 17.2: Source: http://photos.state.gov/galleries/usinfo-photo/39/civil_rights_07/9.html.

Homework

Directions

- Continue to read the letter by Dr. Martin Luther King Jr. that appears on the previous pages.

- Complete the **DOXI** as directed.

- Respond to the two prompts that follow.

Select one **word** (concept) that you would like to better understand from Dr. Martin Luther King Jr.'s letter.

_____

WORD *(concept)*

D: Select the appropriate dictionary **D**efinition (use http://dictionary.reference.com/ or another dictionary).

_____

_____

O: Put this definition into your **O**wn words. (i.e., PARAPHRASE)

_____

_____

X: Give an e**X**ample of this WORD (concept) from your own personal experience.

_____

_____

I: _I_llustrate the WORD (concept). Go online and find an image that captures the meaning of this word.

1. What do you think is the **PROBLEM** that Dr. Martin Luther King Jr. writes about in this letter?

_____

_____

_____

2. What is your **POINT OF VIEW** on the PROBLEM you identified earlier?

_____

_____

_____

_____

Investigation Plan (Begin)

OA Topic

MA Peer Discussion: Topic, Title, and Problem

CA Problem, Purpose, and Title

HW Investigative Article, Part 1—INVESTIGATION PLAN: Draft

"What is worth learning is worth learning well."

—Alfred North Whitehead

Opening Activity

Directions

- As a reflection on the **Investigative Article** you wrote, briefly describe how creating a "specific" **TOPIC** helped you carry out your investigation.

_____

_____

_____

_____

_____

Main Activity

You will write an **Investigative Article** over the next ten class sessions. This article will consist of three parts: **INVESTIGATION PLAN, INVESTIGATION RESEARCH**, and **INVESTIGATION FINDINGS**.

Our work now will focus on your **INVESTIGATION PLAN**.

Directions

- Based on your reflection in the "Opening Activity," identify and write one "specific" **TOPIC** in either **history** <u>or</u> **philosophy** (from Classes #15–#17) that you would be interested in investigating and writing about.

- Review the **TOPIC** Tool (the "<u>W</u>" version) as you prepare to investigate the "specific" **TOPIC** you chose.

Write what will be the "specific" **TOPIC** of focus for yourinvestigation:

_____

_____

TOPIC TOOL	<u>W</u> Select a specific topic to be the focus of your writing.

Use the four criteria that follow to review the "specific **TOPIC**" your partner came up with. Then have a "<u>peer discussion</u>" with your partner to give recommendations to help one another make your "specific" **TOPICS** clear, focused, important, and practical:

Criteria (for Peer Discussion)

➤ <u>Clear</u>: Does the **TOPIC** make clear what is to be investigated?

➤ <u>Focused</u>: Is the **TOPIC** as focused ("specific") as it needs to be?

➤ <u>Important</u>: Is there a need to investigate this **TOPIC**?

➤ <u>Practical</u>: Is this investigation practical to complete in the given time frame?

<u>"Peer Discussion"</u>

Peer Ideas (Recommendation)

Rewrite your partner's **TOPIC** in light of theese four criteria:

_____

_____

_____

As a final step, now rewrite the **TOPIC** you will investigate:

_____

_____

_____

Closing Activity

Directions

▪ To prepare to write your **INVESTIGATION PLAN** for the "specific" **TOPIC** you chose, respond to the **prompts** that follow.

1. The specific **TOPIC** I will focus on is:

_____

2. The main **PROBLEM** I will focus on in my investigation is:

_____

_____

I think this is an important **PROBLEM** to investigate because ...

_____

_____

_____

PROBLEM TOOL	<u>W</u> Identify the main problem or issue that is the focus of your writing. Explain why this is a problem.

3. The **PURPOSE** of my investigation is:

_____

_____

_____

PURPOSE TOOL	<u>W</u> Explain what you want to accomplish through your writing.

4. The "working" **TITLE** for my investigation is:

_____

TITLE TOOL	<u>W</u> Create a title that expresses the main idea (focus) of your writing.

Homework

Directions

- Fill in the following chart with your ideas for your "working" **INVESTIGATION PLAN** to be reviewed at our next class meeting.

- To do this, use what you came up with today and then make any further adjustments you think are needed to make the wording even better.

My "Working" **INVESTIGATION PLAN** Ideas

TOPIC	
TITLE	
PROBLEM	
PURPOSE	

Investigation Plan (Continued)

OA   Question Creation

MA   INVESTIGATION PLAN: Begin Draft

CA   LAB: Information/Review of Literature

HW   INVESTIGATION PLAN: Continue Draft

"What is worth learning is worth learning well."

—Alfred North Whitehead

Opening Activity

Directions

- Review the **QUESTION** Tool (the "<u>W</u>" version) to create two key **QUESTIONS** you will use to focus your investigation.

*Note: Consider turning the "working" **TITLE** you created in Class #18 into the form of a question.*

QUESTION TOOL	<u>W</u> Pose a thought-provoking question(s) you will investigate and address in your writing.

TWO KEY QUESTIONS	Q#1:
	Q#2:

Main Activity

Directions

- Use the two **criteria** that follow to make recommendations about the **QUESTIONS** your partner posed.

Criteria (for Peer Discussion)
➤ <u>Focused</u>: Do your **QUESTIONS** help keep your focus on what to look for?
➤ <u>Practical</u>: Can the search for **INFORMATION** to address and answer these **QUESTIONS** be done in a reasonable amount of time?

<u>"Peer Discussion"</u>

TWO KEY QUESTIONS (PEER RECOMMENDA-TIONS)	Q#1:
	Q#2:

- Revise your **QUESTIONS** based on the recommendations you received from your partner and the class discussion.

<u>Revised Questions:</u>

TWO KEY QUESTIONS (REVISED)	Q#1:
	Q#2:

Directions

- Add your revised **QUESTIONS** to the chart that follows.

- Use what you have on your chart that will guide you as we go to the LAB to write a draft of your **INVESTIGATION PLAN**.

MY "Working" **INVESTIGATION PLAN** Ideas

TOPIC	
TITLE	
PROBLEM	
PURPOSE	
QUESTIONS	

Closing Activity (in LAB)

Directions

- Create a Word document (double-spaced) as shown in the setup that follows to write a draft of your **INVESTIGATION PLAN**.

- Use the directions in parentheses to guide your thoughts for each <u>subsection</u> (e.g., **TOPIC, PROBLEM**).

Note: <u>Subsections</u> provide the structure to follow as you write your paper.

<u>Investigative Article</u>, Part 1—INVESTIGATION PLAN

TITLE

(Make sure your "working" **TITLE** expresses to readers exactly what your investigation is about.)

TOPIC

(State the "specific" **TOPIC** you will investigate and elaborate to let us know why you chose this as the focus of your investigation.)

PROBLEM

(State the **PROBLEM** you will investigate, provide some background about the **PROBLEM**, and make the case for why this needs to be investigated.)

PURPOSE

(State your **PURPOSE** for carrying out this investigation and make clear the importance of what you think you will accomplish through this investigation.)

QUESTION

(State the two **QUESTIONS** you posed for your investigation. Identify sources you think you will look at for information to answer these questions.)

Homework

Directions

▪ Continue to write the draft of your **INVESTIGATION PLAN** in the Word document (double-spaced) you created in class today,

Note: The final version will be handed in at the beginning of Class #20.

▪ Use the directions in parentheses to guide your thoughts for each <u>subsection</u>.

<u>Investigative Article</u>, Part 1—INVESTIGATION PLAN

TITLE

(Make sure your "working" **TITLE** expresses to readers exactly what your investigation is about.)

TOPIC

(State the "specific" **TOPIC** you will investigate and elaborate to let us know why you chose this as the focus of your investigation.)

PROBLEM

(State the **PROBLEM** you will investigate, provide some background about the **PROBLEM**, and make the case for why this needs to be investigated.)

PURPOSE

(State your **PURPOSE** for carrying out this investigation and make clear the importance of what you think you will accomplish through this investigation.)

QUESTION

(State the two **QUESTIONS** you posed for your investigation. Identify sources you think you will look at for information to answer these questions.)

Name: _____

Date: _____

Investigation Plan (Continued) and Investigation Research (Begin)

OA   INVESTIGATION PLAN: Peer Recommendations

MA   Significant Sentences

CA   Information/Review of Literature (Research)

HW   INVESTIGATION PLAN: Finalize to Submit in Class #21

"What is worth learning is worth learning well."

—Alfred North Whitehead

Opening Activity

Directions

- Read your partner's draft of the **INVESTIGATION PLAN** and give your recommendations for each <u>subsection</u> that follows.

<u>Partner</u>

✓ **TOPIC:**

(*State the "specific" **TOPIC** you will investigate and elaborate to let us know **why** you chose this as the focus of your investigation.)

<u>Recommendations</u>:

_____

_____

_____

✓ **PROBLEM:**

(State the **PROBLEM** you will investigate, provide some background about the **PROBLEM**, and make the case for **why** this needs to be investigated.)

<u>Recommendations</u>:

_____

_____

_____

✓ PURPOSE:

(State your **PURPOSE** for carrying out this investigation and make clear the importance of what you think you will accomplish through this investigation.)

Recommendations:

_____

_____

_____

✓ QUESTIONS:

(State the two **QUESTIONS** you posed for your investigation. Identify sources you think you will look at for information to answer these questions.)

Recommendations:

_____

_____

_____

✓ TITLE:

(Make sure your **TITLE** expresses exactly what your investigation is about.)

Recommendations:

_____

_____

_____

Directions

- Discuss your recommendations with your partner.

- Use these recommendations as appropriate to edit your **INVESTIGATION PLAN** and submit your final version at the Class #21 meeting.

Main Activity

Directions

- Review the **SIGNIFICANT SENTENCE** Tool (the "<u>W</u>" version) and then respond to the prompt that follows.

SIGNIFICANT SENTENCE(S) TOOL	<u>W</u> Create sentences that express your thoughts and are important to accomplish the purpose of your writing. Elaborate and give examples to make your thoughts clear.

PROMPT: Revise what you have written for the **PROBLEM** <u>subsection</u> of your **INVESTIGATION PLAN** through the use of the **SIGNIFICANT SENTENCE** Tool. Elaborate with a few examples that you have read or heard about or experienced to illustrate the reality and seriousness of the **PROBLEM** you have chosen to investigate.

PROBLEM (revised)

_____

_____

_____

_____

_____

_____

Closing Activity

Directions

- As a reflection on your experience writing your **Investigative Article**, briefly explain how the **INFORMATION/REVIEW of LITERATURE** Tool (the "<u>W</u>" version) helped you.

_____

_____

_____

_____

_____

- How do you think you can make better use of this tool for future investigations you will carry out?

_____

_____

_____

_____

_____

Directions

- Review the **INFORMATION/REVIEW of LITERATURE** Tool (the "<u>W</u>" version)

INFORMATION/ REVIEW OF LITERATURE TOOL	<u>W</u>	Search for information and ideas to deepen your understanding and support important points you make in your writing. Cite relevant sources accordingly.

- Identify specific **INFORMATION** you think you will need for your investigation. Name <u>two</u> **sources** you will go to for this **INFORMATION** and explain **why** you will look in those sources.

INFORMATION (**what** you search for): _____

_____

_____

_____

_____

_____

_____

_____

Source #1 (**where** you will look): _____

_____

_____

_____

Why will you look there: _____

_____

_____

Source #2 (where you will look): _____

_____

_____

_____

Why will you look there: _____

_____

_____

_____

Homework

Directions

- Finalize your **INVESTIGATION PLAN** to submit at the beginning of Class #21.

Investigative Article, Part 1—INVESTIGATION PLAN

TITLE

(Make sure your "working" **TITLE** expresses to readers exactly what your investigation is about.)

TOPIC

(State the "specific" **TOPIC** you will investigate and elaborate to let us know why you chose this as the focus of your investigation.)

PROBLEM

(State the **PROBLEM** you will investigate, provide some background about the **PROBLEM**, and make the case for why this needs to be investigated.)

PURPOSE

(State your **PURPOSE** for carrying out this investigation and make clear the importance of what you think you will accomplish through this investigation.)

QUESTION

(State the two **QUESTIONS** you posed for your investigation. Identify sources you think you will look at for information to answer these questions.)

Name: _____

Date: _____

Investigation Research (Continued)

INVESTIGATION PLAN—Submit Today

OA   INVESTIGATION RESEARCH: Structure

MA   Speak in the Author's Voice, Paraphrase, and Source Notes

CA   LAB: Begin Research

HW   Investigative Article, Part 2—INVESTIGATION RESEARCH

"What is worth learning is worth learning well."

—Alfred North Whitehead

Opening Activity

Directions

- Under "**INVESTIGATION RESEARCH**," write the name of the <u>subsections</u> you used for this phase of the investigation in your previous **Investigative Article**.

INVESTIGATION RESEARCH

- _____

- _____

- _____

- _____

Directions

▪ Review the list of <u>subsections</u> to use for our **INVESTIGATION RESEARCH**.

▪ In a clear, complete sentence, explain **why** you think each <u>subsection</u> was important to research and write about for the investigation you carried out.

INVESTIGATION RESEARCH

▪ **Background and Significance of the PROBLEM**

Why? _____

_____

_____

_____

▪ **Causes of the PROBLEM**

Why? _____

_____

_____

_____

▪ **Solutions to the PROBLEM**

Why? _____

_____

_____

_____

▪ **Roadblocks to Overcoming the PROBLEM**

Why? _____

_____

_____

_____

Main Activity

Directions

- Review the **SPEAK in the AUTHOR'S VOICE** Tool (the "<u>W</u>" version) and briefly describe how you think the use of this tool will help you carry out your investigation.

_____

_____

_____

_____

SPEAK IN THE AUTHOR'S VOICE TOOL	<u>W</u> Include quotes (or paraphrases of quotes) from selected authors or sources to support and clarify what you want to express in your writing. Cite relevant sources accordingly.

- Review the **PARAPHRASE** Tool (the "<u>W</u>" version) and briefly describe why you would sometimes use this tool instead of a direct quote in your writing.

_____

_____

_____

_____

PARAPHRASE TOOL	<u>W</u> Paraphrase a sentence(s) from what you read to use in your writing.

Directions

- Now that you have completed an **Investigative Article**, how would you respond if a friend asks, "What are two things I should do to take good notes from the sources I find for my investigation?"

_____

_____

_____

_____

Directions

- Review the "source notes" form on the following page as a way to take and organize notes from the sources you find.

- Review its three main features: "**Bibliographic Information**," "**Pg(s)/Para(s)/Line(s)**," and "**Notes (Direct Quotes or Paraphrases)/My Comments and Ideas**."

- Choose **one** of these three features and explain how you think it will help you as you take notes from sources you find.

Feature: _____

How it will help: _____

_____

_____

_____

_____

Source Notes

For: _____

| Bibliographic Information | Date Notes Taken: _____ |

Bibliographic Information   Date Notes Taken: _____

Author(s): _____

Name of Book, Article, Website, (& URL):

_____

Page(s): _____

Publication Date: _____   City, State: _____

Publisher: _____

Pg(s)	Para(s)	Line(s)	Notes (Direct Quotes or Paraphrases)/My Comments and Ideas

Directions

- Read the following descriptions of how to best use each of the three main features of this method for taking source notes.

1. **Bibliographic Information**

   While you are at a particular source (i.e., book, article, website/URL), copy the information that is asked for. This will make sure you can **a)** easily locate this source again and **b)** have what you need for your "References" (or "Work Cited") page. **See NOTE #1**.

2. **Pg(s)/Para(s)/Line(s)**

   Note the exact location in **each source** (i.e., specific pages, paragraphs, and lines) for the direct quotes, paraphrases of quotes, and general references to be able to get right back to this information whenever you need to.

3. **Notes (Direct Quotes or Paraphrases)/My Comments and Ideas**

   Notes:

   Copy the exact notes you want to use in your writing and make clear which are exact quotations (use quotation marks on these) and which are your paraphrases of quotations. **See NOTE #2**.

   My Comments and Ideas:

   Write your thoughts about these specific notes or your own original ideas that this information brings to mind.

NOTE #1: To create your "References" (or "Work Cited") page use the **bibliographic information** you have written down on the **Source Notes** forms and then use the format style (e.g., *MLA*, *APA*, *Chicago*) you are required to follow.

NOTE #2: To use quotations and your paraphrases of quotations in your writing, use the format style (e.g., *MLA*, *APA*, *Chicago*) you are required to follow.

Directions

- Review the example of how these three main features can be used to take source notes from the Rachel Carson Book Excerpt (*Silent Spring*) we read in Class #4.

Source Notes

For: _____

Bibliographic Information	Date Notes Taken: _____

Author(s): *Rachel Carson*

Name of Book, Article, Website, (& URL): *Silent Spring*

Page(s): *?* _____

Publication Date: *1962* _____   City, State: _*New York, NY*_____

Publisher: *Houghton Mifflin* _____

Pg(s)	Para(s)	Line(s)	Notes (Direct Quotes or Paraphrases)/My Comments and Ideas
2	*2*	*5–7*	*Author:* "*The farmers spoke of much illness among their families. In the town the doctors had become more and more puzzled by new kinds of sickness appearing among their patients.*"
2	*2*	*5–7*	*My Comment:* *This quote demonstrates how important it is for people to understand that pollution of the environment kills people and destroys lives.*
2	*2*	*5–7*	*My Idea:* *This makes me want to investigate and find out what one of the main causes of environmental pollution and to find some of the best solutions to overcome this pollution.*

Closing Activity (in LAB)

Directions

- Use the **INFORMATION/REVIEW OF LITERATURE** Tool to carry out research for your investigation.

INFORMATION/ REVIEW OF LITERATURE TOOL	**W** Search for information and ideas to deepen your understanding and support important points you make in your writing. Cite relevant sources accordingly.

- Find two relevant sources that have valuable information to help you write the first <u>subsection</u> of your **INVESTIGATION RESEARCH: Background and Significance of the PROBLEM**

- Complete a "source notes" form for **each source** you find. Write the specific information you think you will use for this <u>subsection</u>.

Source Notes #1

For: Background and Significance of the PROBLEM

| **Bibliographic Information** | Date Notes Taken: _____ |
| Author(s): _____ |
| Name of Book, Article, Website, (& URL): |
| _____ |
| Page(s): _____ |
| Publication Date: _____ | City, State: _____ |
| Publisher: _____ |

Pg(s)	Para(s)	Line(s)	Notes (Direct Quotes or Paraphrases)/My Comments and Ideas

Source Notes #2

For: Background and Significance of the PROBLEM

Bibliographic Information	Date Notes Taken: _____
Author(s): _____	
Name of Book, Article, Website, (& URL):	
_____	
Page(s): _____	
Publication Date: _____	City, State: _____
Publisher: _____	

Pg(s)	Para(s)	Line(s)	Notes (Direct Quotes or Paraphrases)/My Comments and Ideas

Homework

Directions

- Use the **INFORMATION/REVIEW OF LITERATURE** Tool to carry out research for your investigation.

- Find one more relevant source in addition to the two you found in the LAB today for the first <u>subsection</u> of your **INVESTIGATION RESEARCH: Background and Significance of the PROBLEM**.

- Complete a "source notes" form for **each source** you find.

Source Notes #3

For: Background and Significance of the PROBLEM

Bibliographic Information   Date Notes Taken: _____
Author(s): _____
Name of Book, Article, Website, (& URL):
_____
Page(s): _____
Publication Date: _____   City, State: _____
Publisher: _____

Pg(s)	Para(s)	Line(s)	Notes (Direct Quotes or Paraphrases)/My Comments and Ideas

Directions

- Find three relevant sources for the second <u>subsection</u> of your **INVESTIGATION RESEARCH: Causes of the PROBLEM**

- Complete a "source notes" form for **each source** you find.

Source Notes #1

For: Causes of the PROBLEM

Bibliographic Information	Date Notes Taken: _____
Author(s): _____	
Name of Book, Article, Website, (& URL):	
_____	
Page(s): _____	
Publication Date: _____	City, State: _____
Publisher: _____	

Pg(s)	Para(s)	Line(s)	Notes (Direct Quotes or Paraphrases)/My Comments and Ideas

Source Notes #2

For: Causes of the PROBLEM

Bibliographic Information	Date Notes Taken: _____
Author(s): _____	
Name of Book, Article, Website, (& URL):	
_____	
Page(s): _____	
Publication Date: _____	City, State: _____
Publisher: _____	

Pg(s)	Para(s)	Line(s)	Notes (Direct Quotes or Paraphrases)/My Comments and Ideas

Source Notes #3

For: Causes of the PROBLEM

Bibliographic Information	Date Notes Taken: _____

Author(s): _____

Name of Book, Article, Website, (& URL):

_____

Page(s): _____

Publication Date: _____   City, State: _____

Publisher: _____

Pg(s)	Para(s)	Line(s)	Notes (Direct Quotes or Paraphrases)/My Comments and Ideas

Name: _____

Date: _____

Investigation Research (Continued)

OA   Peer Discussion: Source Notes (Review and Recommend)

MA   Peer Discussion: Source Notes (Discuss and Revise)

CA   LAB: INVESTIGATION RESEARCH: Begin Draft of "Background" and "Causes" Subsections

HW   INVESTIGATION RESEARCH: Continue Draft of "Background" and "Causes" Subsections

"What is worth learning is worth learning well."

—Alfred North Whitehead

Opening and Main Activity

Directions

- Use the three criteria that follow to review your partner's "source notes" (**Notes/My Comments and Ideas**) for the "**Background and Significance of the PROBLEM**" and the "**Causes of the PROBLEM**" <u>subsections</u> of their **INVESTIGATION PLAN**.

Criteria (for Peer Discussion)

➤ <u>Clear</u>: Are the **"Notes/My Comments and Ideas"** clearly understandable?

➤ <u>Focused</u>: Are the **"Notes/My Comments and Ideas"** as focused ("specific") as they need to be?

➤ <u>Important</u>: Are the **"Notes/My Comments and Ideas"** important to the PROBLEM investigated?

- Give recommendations to your partner concerning the "sources" and the "information" he or she found.

- Discuss your recommendations with your partner and then revise your "source notes" accordingly.

"Peer Discussion"

Background and Significance of the PROBLEM

<u>Source #1</u>

✓ <u>Recommendations</u> on the value of **Information:**

_____

_____

_____

✓ <u>Recommendations</u> on the value of **Source:**

_____

_____

_____

_____

<u>Source #2</u>

✓ <u>Recommendations</u> on the value of **Information:**

_____

_____

_____

_____

✓ <u>Recommendations</u> on the value of **Source:**

_____

_____

_____

Source #3

✓ <u>Recommendations</u> on the value of **Information:**

_____

_____

_____

✓ <u>Recommendations</u> on the value of **Source:**

_____

_____

_____

Causes of the PROBLEM

Source #1

✓ <u>Recommendations</u> on the value of **Information:**

_____

_____

_____

✓ <u>Recommendations</u> on the value of **Source:**

_____

_____

_____

Source #2

✓ <u>Recommendations</u> on the value of **Information:**

_____

_____

_____

✓ <u>Recommendations</u> on the value of **Source:**

_____

_____

_____

Source #3

✓ <u>Recommendations</u> on the value of **Information:**

_____

_____

_____

✓ <u>Recommendations</u> on the value of **Source:**

_____

_____

_____

Closing Activity (in LAB)

Directions

- Create a Word document (double-spaced) as shown in the setup earlier to write a draft of your **Investigative Article**, Part 2—**INVESTIGATIVE RESEARCH**.

- Use the information you found in your research, along with your own thoughts, to write each <u>subsection</u>.

Note: <u>Subsections</u> provide the structure to follow as you write your paper.

Investigative Article, Part 2—**INVESTIGATIVE RESEARCH**

Background and Significance of the PROBLEM

Causes of the PROBLEM

Homework

Directions

- Continue to write the draft of your **INVESTIGATIVE RESEARCH** in the Word document (double-spaced) you created in class today.

Note: You will submit the final version at the beginning of Class #23.

Name: _____

Date: _____

Investigation Research (Continued)

OA   Peer Discussion: Draft of "Background" and "Causes" Subsections

MA   LAB: Begin Research on "Solutions" and "Roadblocks" Subsections

CA   LAB: Continue Research on "Solutions" and "Roadblocks" Subsections

HW   INVESTIGATION RESEARCH: Continue Draft of "Background" and "Causes" Subsections/Add Draft of "Solutions" and "Roadblocks" Subsections

"What is worth learning is worth learning well."

–Alfred North Whitehead

Opening Activity

Directions

- Have a "peer discussion" with your partner to give recommendations about your partner's draft (Word document) of the **"Background"** and the **"Causes"** <u>subsections</u> of their **INVESTIGATION RESEARCH**.

- Make recommendations to your partner concerning the draft of his or her **"Introduction"** and **"Causes"** <u>subsections</u> in the space provided next.

- Discuss your recommendations with your partner.

- Review and consider your partner's recommendations for possible use as you continue to draft and edit these two <u>subsections</u>.

<u>"Peer Discussion"</u>

✓ **Background and Significance of the PROBLEM**

<u>Recommendations</u>:

_____

_____

_____

_____

✓ **Causes of the PROBLEM**

<u>Recommendations</u>:

_____

_____

_____

_____

Main Activity and Closing Activity (in LAB)

MA CA

Directions

- Use the **INFORMATION/REVIEW OF LITERATURE** Tool to find three relevant sources for the third and the fourth <u>subsections</u> of your **INVESTIGATIVE RESEARCH: Solutions to PROBLEM** and **Roadblocks to Overcoming the PROBLEM**.

INFORMATION/ REVIEW OF LITERATURE TOOL	<u>W</u> Search for information and ideas to deepen your understanding and support important points you make in your writing. Cite relevant sources accordingly.

- Complete a "source notes" form for **each source** you find. Write the specific information you think you will use for this <u>subsection</u>.

Source Notes #1

For: Solutions to PROBLEM

Bibliographic Information	Date Notes Taken:_____
Author(s): _____	
Name of Book, Article, Website, (& URL):	
_____	
Page(s): _____	
Publication Date: _____	City, State: _____
Publisher: _____	

Pg(s)	Para(s)	Line(s)	Notes (Direct Quotes or Paraphrases)/My Comments and Ideas

Source Notes #2

For: Solutions to PROBLEM

Bibliographic Information	Date Notes Taken: _____

Author(s): _____

Name of Book, Article, Website, (& URL):

_____

Page(s): _____

Publication Date: _____ City, State: _____

Publisher: _____

Pg(s)	Para(s)	Line(s)	Notes (Direct Quotes or Paraphrases)/My Comments and Ideas

Source Notes #3

For: Solutions to PROBLEM

Bibliographic Information	Date Notes Taken: _____
Author(s): _____	
Name of Book, Article, Website, (& URL):	
_____	
Page(s): _____	
Publication Date: _____	City, State: _____
Publisher: _____	

Pg(s)	Para(s)	Line(s)	Notes (Direct Quotes or Paraphrases)/My Comments and Ideas

Source Notes #1

For: Roadblocks to Overcoming the PROBLEM

Bibliographic Information	Date Notes Taken: _____

Author(s): _____

Name of Book, Article, Website, (& URL):

_____

Page(s): _____

Publication Date: _____   City, State: _____

Publisher: _____

Pg(s)	Para(s)	Line(s)	Notes (Direct Quotes or Paraphrases)/My Comments and Ideas

Source Notes #2

For: Roadblocks to Overcoming the PROBLEM

Bibliographic Information	Date Notes Taken: _____
Author(s): _____	
Name of Book, Article, Website, (& URL):	
_____	
Page(s): _____	
Publication Date: _____	City, State: _____
Publisher: _____	

Pg(s)	Para(s)	Line(s)	Notes (Direct Quotes or Paraphrases)/My Comments and Ideas

Source Notes #3

For: Roadblocks to Overcoming the PROBLEM

Bibliographic Information	Date Notes Taken: _____
Author(s): _____	
Name of Book, Article, Website, (& URL):	
_____	
Page(s): _____	
Publication Date: _____	City, State: _____
Publisher: _____	

Pg(s)	Para(s)	Line(s)	Notes (Direct Quotes or Paraphrases)/My Comments and Ideas

Homework

Directions

- Continue to write the draft of your **INVESTIGATIVE RESEARCH** by adding the **"Solutions"** and the **"Roadblocks"** <u>subsections</u> to the Word document (double-spaced) you have created.

- Use the information you found in your research, along with your own thoughts, to write each <u>subsection</u>.

Note: You will submit the final version at the beginning of Class #24.

<u>**Investigative Article**, Part 2–**INVESTIGATIVE RESEARCH**</u>

TITLE

Background and Significance of the PROBLEM

Causes of the PROBLEM

Solutions to the PROBLEM

Roadblocks to Overcoming the PROBLEM

Investigation Research (Continued) and Investigation Findings (Begin)

OA Peer Discussion: Draft of "Solutions" and "Roadblocks" Subsections

MA INVESTIGATION FINDINGS

CA LAB: Revise Draft of "Solutions" and "Roadblocks" Subsections

HW INVESTIGATION RESEARCH: Finalize to Submit in Class #25

"What is worth learning is worth learning well."

—Alfred North Whitehead

Opening Activity

Directions

- Have a "peer discussion" with your partner to give recommendations about your partner's draft (Word document) of the **"Solutions"** and the **"Roadblocks"** subsections of his or her **INVESTIGATION RESEARCH**.

- Make recommendations to your partner concerning the draft of his or her **"Solutions"** and the **"Roadblocks"** subsections in the space provided next.

- Discuss your recommendations with your partner.

- Review and consider your partners' recommendations for possible use as you continue to draft and edit these two subsections.

"Peer Discussion"

✓ **Solutions to the PROBLEM**
  Recommendations:

_____

_____

_____

_____

✓ Roadblocks to Overcoming the PROBLEM

Recommendations:

_____

_____

_____

_____

Main Activity

Directions

- Review the **CONCLUSION** Tool (the "<u>W</u>" version) and write one of the most important conclusions you reached about the specific **PROBLEM** as a result of your investigation. Be sure to explain **how** you reached this **CONCLUSION**.

CONCLUSION TOOL	<u>W</u> State the most important conclusion that you come to in your writing and explain how you reached that conclusion.

CONCLUSION #1

_____

_____

_____

_____

_____

- Review the **RECOMMENDATION** Tool (the "<u>W</u>" version) and write one **RECOMMENDATION** for what should be done in light of the CONCLUSION you stated earlier.

RECOMMENDATION TOOL	<u>W</u> State what you think should be done to deal effectively with the main problem or issue you address in your writing.

RECOMMENDATION #1

_____

_____

_____

_____

_____

_____

_____

- Review the **CONSEQUENCES** Tool (the "<u>W</u>" version) and state one thing you think will happen if we <u>do follow</u> the RECOMMENDATION you made earlier and one thing that will happen if we <u>do not</u> follow this RECOMMENDATION.

CONSEQUENCES TOOL	<u>W</u> State what you think could happen if we follow or do not follow what you recommend or imply in your writing.

CONSEQUENCES

_____

_____

_____

_____

_____

> **CONCLUSIONS, RECOMMENDATIONS,** and **CONSEQUENCES** will be the three subsections for the last part of your **Investigative Article, INVESTIGATION FINDINGS**.

Closing Activity (in LAB)

Directions

- Revise the "**Solutions**" and "**Roadblocks**" <u>subsections</u> in preparation to finalize your **INVESTIGATION RESEARCH** to submit at the beginning of next class, Class #25.

Homework

Directions

▪ Finalize your **INVESTIGATION RESEARCH** to submit at the beginning of Class #25.

<u>**Investigative Article**</u>, Part 2—**INVESTIGATIVE RESEARCH**

TITLE

Background and Significance of the PROBLEM

Causes of the PROBLEM

Solutions to the PROBLEM

Roadblocks to Overcoming the PROBLEM

Name: _____

Date: _____

Investigation Findings (Continued)

INVESTIGATION RESEARCH—Submit Today

OA   INVESTIGATION FINDINGS: Structure

MA   LAB: INVESTIGATION FINDINGS: Begin Draft

CA   LAB: Peer Discussion: Draft of "Conclusions," "Recommendations," and "Consequences" Subsections

HW   Investigative Article, Part 3—INVESTIGATION FINDINGS: Draft

"What is worth learning is worth learning well."

—Alfred North Whitehead

Opening Activity

At this point, you have created an **INVESTIGATION PLAN** that focused on a specific PROBLEM and looked into this through your **INVESTIGATION RESEARCH**.

To complete your **Investigative Article**, you will write about what you found and what you think this means. This will be your **INVESTIGATION FINDINGS**.

Directions

- Use the **CONCLUSION** Tool (the "<u>W</u>" version) to write one more important **CONCLUSION** in addition to the one you reached during the last class.

CONCLUSION TOOL	**W** State the most important conclusion that you come to in your writing and explain how you reached that conclusion.

CONCLUSION #2

_____

_____

_____

_____

_____

▪ Use the **RECOMMENDATION** Tool (the "<u>W</u>" version) to write one more **RECOMMENDATION** in addition to the one you gave during the last class.

RECOMMENDATION TOOL	<u>W</u> State what you think should be done to deal effectively with the main problem or issue you address in your writing.

RECOMMENDATION #2

_____

_____

_____

_____

_____

▪ Use the **CONSEQUENCES** Tool (the "<u>W</u>" version) to elaborate further on what you wrote in the last class about what you think will happen if we do follow your RECOMMENDATIONS <u>or</u> do not follow your RECOMMENDATIONS

CONSEQUENCES TOOL	<u>W</u> State what you think could happen if we follow or do not follow what you recommend or imply in your writing.

CONSEQUENCES

_____

_____

_____

_____

_____

Main Activity (in LAB)

Directions

- Create a Word document (double-spaced) as shown in the setup that follows to write a draft of your **Investigative Article**, Part 3—**INVESTIGATIVE FINDINGS**.

- Use what you have already written for **CONCLUSIONS**, **RECOMMENDATIONS**, and **CONSEQUENCES** for these <u>subsections</u>.

Note: <u>*Subsections*</u> *provide the structure to follow as you write your paper.*

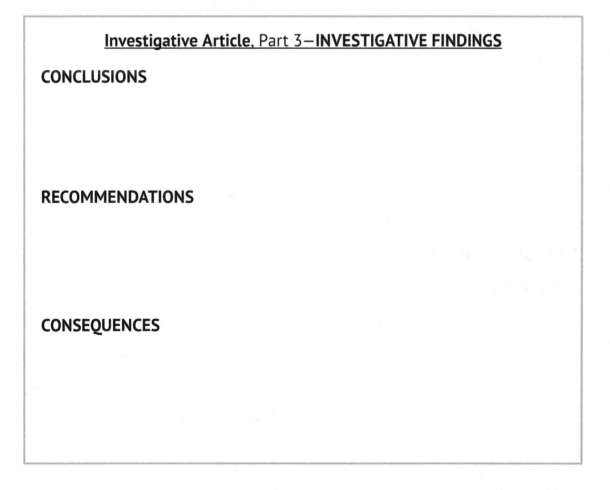

<u>**Investigative Article**</u>, Part 3—**INVESTIGATIVE FINDINGS**

CONCLUSIONS

RECOMMENDATIONS

CONSEQUENCES

Closing Activity (in LAB)

Directions

- Have a "peer discussion" with your partner to give recommendations about your partner's draft (Word document) of the **"CONCLUSIONS," "RECOMMENDA-TIONS,"** and **"CONSEQUENCES"** <u>subsections</u> of their **INVESTIGATION FINDINGS**.

- Discuss your recommendations with your partner.

- Review and consider your partners' recommendations for possible use as you continue to draft and edit these three <u>subsections</u>.

<u>"Peer Discussion"</u>

✓ CONCLUSIONS

<u>Recommendations</u>:

_____

_____

_____

_____

✓ RECOMMENDATIONS

<u>Recommendations</u>:

_____

_____

_____

_____

✓ CONSEQUENCES

<u>Recommendations</u>:

_____

_____

_____

_____

Homework

Directions

- Continue to write the draft of your **INVESTIGATIVE FINDINGS** in the Word document (double-spaced) you created in class today.

Note: You will submit the final version at the beginning of Class #27.

Name: _____

Date: _____

Investigation Findings (Continued)

OA Peer Discussion: Draft of INVESTIGATION FINDINGS

MA Preparation of Abstract for Presentation

CA LAB: Revise Draft of INVESTIGATION FINDINGS

HW INVESTIGATION FINDINGS: Finalize to Submit in Class #27/
Create Abstract to Present

*"What is worth learning is
worth learning well."*

—Alfred North Whitehead

Opening Activity

- Have a "peer discussion" with your partner to read and give your ideas about your partner's draft of each <u>subsection</u> for his or her **INVESTIGATION FINDINGS** in the space provided next.

- Discuss your ideas with your partner.

- Review and consider your partner's ideas for possible use as you continue to edit and finalize these three subsections of your **INVESTIGATION FINDINGS**.

CONCLUSIONS

Idea(s) to Consider:

_____

_____

_____

_____

_____

RECOMMENDATIONS

Idea(s) to Consider:

_____

_____

_____

_____

_____

CONSEQUENCES

Idea(s) to Consider:

_____

_____

_____

_____

_____

Main Activity

Directions

- At our next class meeting (Class #27) you will submit your **INVESTIGATION FINDINGS** and an "abstract" of your **INVESTIGATIVE Article.**

- Create a Word document as shown in the setup that follows to write the _one-page_ "abstract" of your **INVESTIGATIVE Article.**

- You will briefly (three minutes maximum) present your "abstract" to the class using the document camera.

Name: _____

INVESTIGATIVE Article—ABSTRACT
TITLE

Specific **PROBLEM** Investigated

_____

_____

_____

_____

_____

_____

Most Important **CONCLUSIONS** Reached

_____

_____

_____

_____

_____

_____

Most Important **RECOMMENDATIONS**

_____

_____

_____

_____

_____

_____

Closing Activity (in LAB)

Directions

- Continue to work on your **INVESTIGATIVE FINDINGS**.
- Create your one-page "abstract."

Homework

Directions

- Finalize your **INVESTIGATION FINDINGS** for submission and your "abstract" for presentation during Class #27.

Investigative Article: Abstract Presentations

INVESTIGATION FINDINGS—Submit Today

OA PRESENTATIONS

MA PRESENTATIONS

CA PRESENTATIONS

HW Think About Questions Posed

"What is worth learning is worth learning well."

—Alfred North Whitehead

Opening, Main, and Closing Activities

Directions

- Present the "abstract" of your **Investigative Article** (three minutes maximum).
- Next, write a thought-provoking question that comes to your mind that you would really like an answer to for four of the presentations (include the name of the presenter with your question).

Question:

_____

_____

_____

       (presenter #1: _____)

Question:

_____

_____

_____

       (presenter #2: _____)

Question:

_____

_____

_____

    (presenter #3: _____)

Question:

_____

_____

_____

    (presenter #4: _____)

Homework

Directions:

- Think about the questions your classmates posed for your investigation.

- Put the Word documents you created for your INVESTIGATION PLAN, INVESTIGATION RESEARCH, and INVESTIGATION FINDINGS into a single Word document. This will be your **Investigative Article** and submit.

PART III

SCIENCE
AND
PSYCHOLOGY

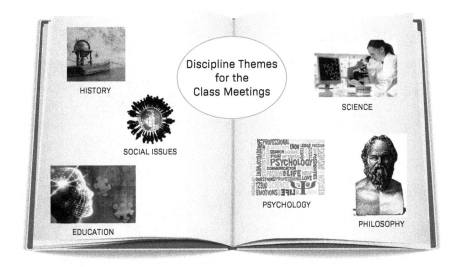

HISTORY

SOCIAL ISSUES

EDUCATION

Discipline Themes
for the
Class Meetings

SCIENCE

PSYCHOLOGY

PHILOSOPHY

Name: _____

Date: _____

Analysis of Textbook Excerpt *The Silent Epidemic*: *Coal and the Hidden Threat to Health* and News Article

OA   Quote, Albert Einstein

MA   Biology Textbook Excerpt

CA   Magazine Article

HW   News Article, Chris Bowman

"What is worth learning is worth learning well."

—Alfred North Whitehead

Opening Activity

Directions

- **PARAPHRASE** the following quote in one clear and complete sentence.

"If you can't explain it simply, you don't understand it well enough."

—Albert Einstein

_____

_____

_____

_____

Main Activity

Directions

- Read the biology textbook excerpt that appears on the following page.
- Use OUR THINKING TOOLBOX to respond to the following **prompts.**

1. What do you think is the main **PROBLEM** discussed in this biology textbook excerpt?

_____

_____

_____

PROBLEM TOOL	**R** Identify the main problem or issue focused on in the reading. Explain why this is a problem.

2. The author's **PURPOSE** in writing these words was ...

_____

_____

_____

PURPOSE TOOL	**R** Explain what you think the author wanted to accomplish through this reading.

3. Underline what you think is the most **SIGNIFICANT SENTENCE** in this excerpt and explain **why** you selected this as the most significant sentence.

_____

_____

_____

SIGNIFICANT SENTENCE(S) TOOL	**R** Select the sentence(s) you think is the most important in the reading and tell why you selected it.

4. What do you think is one possible **CONSEQUENCE** if countries continue to use coal as a main source of energy?

_____

_____

_____

CONSEQUENCE TOOL	**R** State what you think could happen if we follow or do not follow what the author or someone in the reading recommends or implies that we do.

5. Create a **TITLE** for this reading and write it in the box on the following page.

TITLE TOOL	**R** Create a title that expresses the main idea (focus) of the reading.

> **Title:**

By Alan H. Lockwood

Koyaanisqatsi: from the Hopi language, life out of balance.

This Hopi word provides us with a good description of what happens when people are exposed to coal-derived air pollutants—the normal states of equilibrium that characterize essential biochemical and physiological processes are pushed out of balance by the stresses imposed by pollutants. Imbalance disrupts cellular functions and leads to the production of symptoms, tissue injury, and disease. This is the essence of how pollution leads to disease. The devil is in the details.

The air pollution that arises as a result of burning coal is a complex mixture of gases, liquid droplets, and particles [...]. [...] [T]his mix leads to many diverse disorders that range from acute attacks of asthma associated with high ambient ozone levels to the possibility that particulates contribute to the development of neurodegenerative diseases, such as Alzheimer's disease. While the exact mechanisms that cause an exposure to result in a disease are, in many cases, extremely complex and incompletely understood, recent evidence suggests that oxidative stress and inflammation play central roles for many of these.

The Central Role of the Lung

Although there are clear exceptions, inhalation is the primary means by which we are exposed to most air pollutants. This should come as no surprise. The lung is the organ where oxygen is taken up by the body and carbon dioxide is excreted. This carbon dioxide is produced by the metabolism of sugars and other molecules in various body organs. Humans require lots of oxygen and produce lots of carbon dioxide; therefore the surface area of the alveoli, the site of the gas exchange, must be correspondingly large. The volume of air that moves in and out of the lungs must also be large. The interface between alveolar air and the body is where the action begins.

The exposure to airborne pollutants is higher in children than adults. There are several explanations for this increase. According to a review by Bateson and Schwartz, the susceptibility of children to the effects of air pollution is multifactorial and includes the following: (1) Children have different patterns of breathing than adults. (2) They are predominantly mouth-breathers, thereby bypassing the filtering effects of the nasal passages. This allows pollutants to travel deeper into the lungs. (3) They have a larger lung surface area per unit weight than adults. (4) They spend more time out of doors, particularly in the afternoons and during the summer months when ozone and other pollutant levels are likely to be the highest. (5) Children also have higher ventilation rates than adults. They breathe more frequently and breathe more air per unit weight than adults. (6) When active, children may ignore early symptoms of exposure and fail to seek treatment or reduce their exposure by moving to a less polluted environment, such as moving indoors. In addition the diameter of the airways in children is smaller than in adults, and therefore airways may be more susceptible to the effects of the airway narrowing that is characteristic of asthmatic attacks. These factors, combined with the possible adverse impact of pollutants on lung development and the immaturity of enzyme and immune systems that detoxify pollutants, may all contribute.

Closing Activity

Directions

- You are a newspaper editor, and one of your reporters just handed you this short article that she wrote about lipstick. In your role as editor, do the following:

1. Tell your reporter the **TITLE** you are going to give to her story.

TITLE TOOL	**R** Create a title that expresses the main idea (focus) of the reading.

2. Next, write a thought-provoking **QUESTION** for your reporter to use to continue her investigation of the problem presented in this article.

_____

_____

_____

QUESTION TOOL	**R** Pose a thought-provoking question(s) to the author about something that caught your attention in the reading.

Title:

This year, millions of kids' toys were recalled after lead was found in them. Now a new study shows that more than half of the 33 red lipsticks tested from drug and department store brands contained detectable levels of lead, a proven neurotoxin in humans. One-third of them exceeded the Food and Drug Administration's level for lead in candy. As it turns out, the FDA—which regulates the beauty industry—has no pre-market approval authority over cosmetics and can only ask for a product recall, not demand it. And manufacturers don't have to file data on ingredients or report injuries. "Nearly 90% of over the 10,000 chemicals used in cosmetics have not been evaluated for safety" says Stacy Malkan of the Campaign for Safe Cosmetics, which conducted the study. Critics of the study assert that any trace amounts of lead ingested from red lipsticks would be harmless.

To learn which brands are lead-free, go to *Parade.com*

Figure 28.1: Source: http://pixabay.com/en/lipstick-cosmetics-makeup-girl-red-149647/.

Homewok

Directions

- Read the article that appears after the five prompts.
- Respond to the **prompts** that follow in clear, complete sentences.

1. What is the main **PROBLEM** raised by Chris Bowman in this article? Explain **why** you think this is a problem.

_____

_____

_____

PROBLEM TOOL	<u>R</u> Identify the main problem or issue focused on in the reading. Explain why this is a problem.

2. What **RECOMMENDATION** would you make to solve the problem that Chris Bowman raises in the reading?

_____

_____

_____

RECOMMENDATION TOOL	<u>R</u> State what you think should be done to deal effectively with the main problem or issue addressed in the reading.

3. Before reading this article, what **ASSUMPTION** did you have about how careful the state of California is in safeguarding children's health?

_____

_____

_____

ASSUMPTION TOOL	R Identify what you think the author takes for granted (i.e., accepts as true without proof) in the reading.

4. Based on the responses you gave to Prompts #1, 2, and 3, write a one-paragraph message to parents about how they can work together to create greater awareness in the community of this problem. This article on lunch boxes, along with your message, will be printed in the local elementary school Parent-Teacher Association newsletter.

_____

_____

_____

_____

_____

_____

_____

_____

5. Create a **TITLE** for this article and write it in the box on the following page.

TITLE TOOL	**R** Create a title that expresses the main idea (focus) of the reading.

Headline:

By Chris Bowman

THE SACRAMENTO BEE
September 27, 2007

SACRAMENTO—Tens of thousands of state-issued lunchboxes in California promoting healthful eating would have carried warnings about toxic lead on the vinyl surfaces but the state's supplier intervened, according to a company e-mail obtained by *The Sacramento Bee*.

Had the coolers carried the warning labels, state health officials said they would have rejected the shipments from supplier You Name It Promotions Inc. of Oakland. "There would be no way that any product that might require that notice would be acceptable for us to distribute," said Dr. Mark Horton, the state's public health director.

Andrew Halim, vice president of T-A Creations, the Los Angeles based producer of the shoulder-bag-style lunchboxes, said the company, on the advice of its lawyers, began routinely attaching the lead warning on its vinyl lunchboxes in 2006, even if samples showed no significant amounts of the contaminant.

"We put the labels on for our protection from liability," Halim said.

In the case of the custom order for the state's promotional green lunchboxes, however, the company went against its legal advice and omitted the warning tags at the insistence of the state's supplier, You Name It Promotions, Halim said.

Halim shared with the *Bee* a Sept. 19, 2006, e-mail from the supplier instructing his company not to attach the warning.

"Now, we need to be very clear that you understand there can be NO label inside the bag other than the one we created. ... There can be NO label stating this product may contain lead. ... This client (the state) has the lead (testing) report and is satisfied with the results. It would look very odd to see the warning label when they have been supplied good test results," the e-mail said.

As it turned out, some of the giveaway bags later tested positive for high levels of lead, which can be absorbed by food and accumulate in the bloodstream. Lead can impair mental and physical development, especially in children.

State health officials warned consumers last Thursday not to use the 56,000 green lunchboxes after confirming Sacramento County findings that some of the bags contained "elevated" levels of lead. The boxes have been distributed at schools and health fairs as part of a state nutrition-education program.

The state's action prompted a recall from T-A Creations, which promised to refund the supplier on returns.

As a precaution, state health officials warned against the use of an additional 246,000 of its promotional lunchboxes—all colored blue—which are undergoing lead tests.

Marla Kaye, president of You Name It Promotions, defended the company's stance, pointing out that T-A Creations' testing did not show elevated lead levels.

CLASS #29

Analysis of Book Excerpt from Norman Cousins

OA   Quote, Henri Poincaré

MA   Book Excerpt, Norman Cousins

CA   News Article

HW   Article, Student Selected

"What is worth learning is worth learning well."

—Alfred North Whitehead

Opening Activity

Directions

- **PARAPHRASE** the following quote in one clear and complete sentence.

"Science is built of facts the way a house is built of bricks; but an accumulation of facts is no more science than a pile of bricks is a house."
—Henri Poincaré (great French mathematician and scientist)

_____

_____

_____

_____

Main Activity

Directions

- Read the excerpt from Norman Cousins that appears after the six prompts.
- Respond to the four **prompts** that follow.

1. Create a **TITLE** for this excerpt from Norman Cousins and write it in the box at the top of the following page.

_____

_____

TOPIC TOOL	<u>R</u> Identify the specific topic that the author has written about.

2. Tell what you think Norman Cousins' **PURPOSE** was in writing this excerpt.

_____

_____

_____

PURPOSE TOOL	<u>R</u> Explain what you think the author wanted to accomplish through this reading.

3. Select what you think is the most **SIGNIFICANT SENTENCE** in this reading and then explain **why** you selected this sentence.

_____

_____

_____

SIGNIFICANT SENTENCE(S) TOOL	**R** Select the sentence(s) you think is the most important in the reading and tell why you selected it.

4. Pose a thought-provoking **QUESTION** to Norman Cousins that comes to your mind as a result of reading his words.

_____

_____

_____

QUESTION TOOL	**R** Pose a thought-provoking question(s) to the author about something that caught your attention in the reading.

5. What do you think is one **CONCLUSION** Norman Cousins reaches about how much Americans focus on pain relief?

_____

_____

_____

CONCLUSION TOOL	<u>R</u> Identify what you think is the most important conclusion that the author came to in the reading and how that conclusion was reached.

6. Copy the sentences (INFORMATION) that made you think this was the most important **CONCLUSION** Norman Cousins reached in this book excerpt.

_____

_____

_____

_____

INFORMATION/ REVIEW OF LITERATURE TOOL	<u>R</u> Identify information and ideas that support and illustrate important points made by the author in the reading.

Title: _____

By Norman Cousins

Americans are probably the most pain-conscious people on the face of the earth. For years we have had it drummed into us—in print, on radio, over television, in everyday conversation—that any hint of pain is to be banished as though it were the ultimate evil. As a result, we are becoming a nation of pill-grabbers and hypochondriacs, escalating the slightest ache into a searing ordeal.

We know very little about pain and what we don't know makes it hurt all the more. Indeed, no form of illiteracy in the United States is so widespread or costly as ignorance about pain—what it is, what causes it, how to deal with it without panic. Almost everyone can rattle off the names of at least a dozen drugs that can deaden pain from every conceivable cause—all the way from headaches to hemorrhoids. There is far less knowledge about the fact that about 90 percent of pain is self-limiting, that it is not always an indication of poor health, and that, most frequently, it is the result of tension, stress, worry, idleness, boredom, frustration, suppressed rage, insufficient sleep, overeating, poorly balanced diet, smoking, excessive drinking, inadequate exercise, stale air, or any of the other abuses encountered by the human body in modern society.

The most ignored fact of all about pain is that the best way to eliminate it is to eliminate the abuse. Instead, many people reach almost instinctively for the painkillers—aspirins, barbiturates, codeines, tranquilizers, sleeping pills, and dozens of other analgesics or desensitizing drugs.

Most doctors are profoundly troubled over the extent to which the medical profession today is taking on the trappings of a pain-killing industry. Their offices are overloaded with people who are morbidly but mistakenly convinced that something dreadful is about to happen to them. It is all too evident that the campaign to get people to run to a doctor at the first sign of pain has boomeranged. Physicians find it difficult to give adequate attention to patients genuinely in need of expert diagnosis and treatment because their time is soaked up by people who have nothing wrong with them except a temporary indisposition or a psychogenic ache.

Patients tend to feel indignant and insulted if the physician tells them he can find no organic cause for the pain. They tend to interpret the term "psychogenic" to mean that they are complaining of nonexistent symptoms. They need to be educated about the fact that many forms of pain have no underlying physical cause but are the result, as mentioned earlier, of tension, stress, or hostile factors in the general environment. Sometimes a pain may be a manifestation of "conversion hysteria," as mentioned earlier, the name given by Jean Charcot to physical symptoms that have their origins in emotional disturbances.

Obviously, it is folly for an individual to ignore symptoms that could be a warning of a potentially serious illness. Some people are so terrified of getting bad news from a doctor that they allow their malaise to worsen, sometimes past the point of no return. Total neglect is not the answer to hypochondria. The only answer has to be increased education about the way the human body works, so that more people will be able to steer an intelligent course between promiscuous pill-popping and irresponsible disregard of genuine symptoms.

Of all forms of pain, none is more important for the individual to understand than the "threshold" variety. Almost everyone has a telltale ache that is triggered whenever tension or a fatigue reaches a certain point. It can take the form of a migraine-type headache or a squeezing pain deep in the abdomen or cramps or a pain in the lower back or even pain in the joints. The individual who has learned how to make the correlation between such threshold pains and their cause doesn't panic when they occur; he or she does something about relieving the stress and tension. Then, if the pain persists despite the absence of apparent cause, the individual will telephone the doctor.

If ignorance about the nature of pain is widespread, ignorance about the way pain-killing drugs work is even more so. What is not generally understood is that many of the vaunted pain-killing drugs conceal the pain without correcting the underlying condition. They deaden the mechanism in the body that alerts the brain to the fact that something may be wrong. The body can pay a high price for suppression of pain without regard to its basic cause.

Professional athletes are sometimes severely disadvantaged by trainers whose job it is to keep them in action. The more famous the athlete, the greater the risk that he or she may be subjected to extreme medical measures when injury strikes. The star baseball pitcher whose arm is sore because of a torn muscle or tissue damage may need sustained rest more than anything else. But his team is battling for a place in the World Series; so the trainer or team doctor, called upon to work his magic, reaches for a strong dose of butazolidine or other powerful pain suppressants. Presto, the pain disappears! The pitcher takes his place on the mound and does superbly. That could be the last game, however, in which he is able to throw a ball with full strength. The drugs didn't repair the torn muscle or cause the damaged tissue to heal. What they did was to mask the pain, enabling the pitcher to throw hard, further damaging the torn muscle. Little wonder that so many star athletes are cut down in their prime, more the victims of overzealous treatment of their injuries than of the injuries themselves.

The king of all painkillers, of course, is aspirin. The U. S. Food and Drug Administration permits aspirin to be sold without prescription, but the drug, contrary to popular belief, can be dangerous and, in sustained doses, potentially lethal. Aspirin is self-administered by more people than any other drug in the world. Some people are aspirin-poppers, taking ten or more a day. What they don't know is that the smallest dose can cause internal bleeding.

Even more serious perhaps is the fact that aspirin is antagonistic to collagen which has a key role in the formation of connective tissue. Since many forms of arthritis involve disintegration of the connective tissue, the steady use of aspirin can actually intensify the underlying arthritic condition.

The reason why aspirin is prescribed so widely for arthritic patients is that it has an anti-inflammatory effect, apart from its pain-deadening characteristics. In recent years, however, medical researchers have suggested that the anti-inflammatory value of aspirin may be offset by the harm it causes to the body's vital chemistry. Doctors I. Hirsh, D. Street, J. F. Cade, and H. Amy, in the March 1973 issue of the professional journal Blood, showed that aspirin impedes the interaction between "platelet release" and connective tissue. In the Annals of Rheumatic Diseases, also in March 1973, Dr. P. N. Sperryn reported a significant blood loss in patients who were on heavy daily doses of aspirin. (It is not unusual for patients suffering from serious rheumatoid arthritis to take as many as twenty-four aspirin tablets a day.) Again, I call attention to the article in the May 8, 1971 issue of Lancet, the English medical journal. Dr. M. A. Sahud and Dr. R. J. Cohen stated that the systematic use of aspirin by rheumatoid patients produces abnormally low plasma-ascorbic-acid levels. The authors reported that aspirin block the "uptake of ascorbic acid into the blood platelets." Since vitamin C is essential in collagen formation, its depletion by aspirin would seem to run directly counter to the body's need to combat connective tissue breakdown in arthritic conditions. The Lancet article concludes that, at the very least, ascorbic acid should be administered along with aspirin to counteract its harmful effects.

Aspirin is not the only pain-killing drug, of course, that is known to have dangerous side effects. Dr. Daphne A. Poe, of Cornell University, at a medical meeting in New York City in 1974 presented startling evidence of a wide range of hazards associated with sedatives and other pain suppressants. Some of these drugs seriously interfere with the ability of the body to metabolize food properly, producing malnutrition. In some instances, there is also the danger of bone-marrow depression, interfering with the ability of the body to replenish its blood supply.

Pain-killing drugs are among the greatest advances in the history of medicine. Properly used, they can be a boon in alleviating suffering and in treating disease. But their indiscriminate and promiscuous use is making psychological cripples and chronic ailers out of millions of people. The unremitting barrage of advertising for pain-killing drugs, especially over television, has set the stage for a mass anxiety neurosis. Almost from the moment children are old enough to sit upright in front of a television screen, they are being indoctrinated into the hypochondriac's clamorous and morbid world. Little wonder so many people fear pain more than death itself.

It might be a good idea if concerned physicians and educators could get together to make knowledge about pain an important part of the regular school curriculum. As for the populace at large, perhaps some of the same techniques used by public-service agencies to make people cancer-conscious can be used to counteract the growing terror of pain and illness in general. People ought to know that nothing is more remarkable about the human body than its recuperative drive, given a modicum of respect. If our broadcasting stations cannot provide equal time for responses to the pain-killing advertisements, they might at least set aside a few minutes each day for common-sense remarks on the subject of pain. As for the Food and Drug Administration, it might be interesting to know why an agency that has so energetically warned the American people against taking vitamins without prescriptions is doing so little to control over-the-counter sales each year of billions of pain-killing pills, some of which cause more harm than the pain they are supposed to suppress.

Source: Norman Cousins, *Anatomy of an Illness as Perceived by the Patient: Reflections on Healing and Regeneration*, pp. 89-95. Copyright © 2001 by W. W. Norton & Company, Inc. Reprinted with permission.

Closing Activity

Figure 29.1: Copyright © Depositphotos/monkeybusiness.

Directions

- Read the following short newspaper article.
- Respond to the **prompt** that follows.

Public School Students Flunk Physical Fitness

More than two in three public school students in the state are out of shape, according to the latest scores for the California Physical Fitness Test released by the state.

Only 27.1 percent of California students in fifth grade, 30.9 percent in seventh grade and 30.1 percent in ninth grade met six fitness standards.

In San Diego County, less than one-third of fifth-graders and ninth-graders met all six standards, while a little more than one-third of seventh-graders met all of them.

There were some highlights around the county. In Del Mar Union School District, nearly two-thirds of fifth-graders met all the fitness standards. In Rancho Santa Fe, nearly 75 percent met all of them.

Other high-performing school districts included those in Cardiff, Solana Beach and Poway.

Source: U-T San Diego, "Public School Students Flunk Physical Fitness," *U-T San Diego*. Copyright © 2007 by The San Diego Union-Tribune, LLC. Reprinted with permission.

What is one **CONCLUSION** you make based on this short article?

_____

_____

_____

_____

Homework

Directions

- Select an article that focuses on a science-related topic that is of particular interest to you.

- Read the article.

- Use OUR THINKING TOOLBOX to respond to the **prompts** that follow.

1. I think the author's **PURPOSE** in writing this article was ...

_____

_____

_____

PURPOSE TOOL	R Explain what you think the author wanted to accomplish through this reading.

2. What specific **PROBLEM** is pointed out in this science article?

_____

_____

_____

PROBLEM TOOL	**R** Identify the main problem or issue focused on in the reading. Explain why this is a problem.

3. What do you **RECOMMEND** to effectively deal with the PROBLEM presented in the article?

_____

_____

_____

RECOMMENDATION TOOL	**R** State what you think should be done to deal effectively with the main problem or issue addressed in the reading.

4. To what extent has this article made you think about this topic and raised questions that you find valuable for investigating the problem further? Explain **why** you say this.

_____

_____

_____

_____

_____

_____

Analysis of Book Excerpts

"What is worth learning is worth learning well."

—Alfred North Whitehead

Opening Activity

Directions

- Read the quote from the film *The King's Speech* that follows.
- **PARAPHRASE** this quote.
- Respond to the question that follows.

> "My job was to give them faith in their voice and to let them know that a friend was listening."
>
> —*King's Speech (Directed by Tom Hooper, 2010)*

_____

_____

_____

- If a teacher thought this way about her or his students, what effect do you think it would have on those students' learning? Explain **why** you say this.

_____

_____

_____

_____

_____

_____

_____

Main Activity

Directions

- Read the book excerpt by Dr. John E. Sarno, which appears after the five prompts.
- Respond to the five **prompts** that follow.

1. Create a **TITLE** for this book excerpt and write it in the box at the top of the page where the reading begins.

TITLE TOOL	R Create a title that expresses the main idea (focus) of the reading.

2. What do you think Dr. Sarno's **PURPOSE** was in writing this excerpt?

_____

_____

_____

PURPOSE TOOL	R Explain what you think the author wanted to accomplish through this reading.

3. <u>Underline</u> what you think is the most significant sentence in this reading. Next, tell **why** you selected this sentence.

_____

_____

_____

SIGNIFICANT SENTENCE(S) TOOL	<u>R</u> Select the sentence(s) you think is the most important in the reading and tell why you selected it.

4. Pose a thought-provoking **QUESTION** to Dr. Sarno to which you would really like to have an answer about this book excerpt.

_____

_____

_____

QUESTION TOOL	<u>R</u> Pose a thought-provoking question(s) to the author about something that caught your attention in the reading.

5. In a short paragraph, tell what you think would be one **CONSEQUENCE** if those leading the health-care system in the United States took Dr. Sarno's ideas seriously. Explain **why** you say this.

_____

_____

_____

_____

_____

_____

_____

CONSEQUENCE TOOL	**R** State what you think could happen if we follow or do not follow what the author or someone in the reading recommends or implies that we do.

Title: _____

By John E. Sarno, M.D.

I remember the first time John R came into my clinic in 1996. He was a successful business-man in his early forties, well dressed and fit, radiating confidence. He seemed altogether at ease and self-assured—until he bent to sit down. Abruptly his movements slowed and he became so cautious, so fragile, so tentative that he was suddenly a caricature of the driving, confident man who strode through my door only moments before. His body language made it clear that he was either experiencing excruciating pain or feared the pain would strike him if he made the slightest wrong move.

As a medical doctor, I could empathize with his suffering. My specialty is mindbody disorders, and I see cases like this every working day. I hoped I could help him, which meant helping him to help himself, because with mindbody disorders, a doctor cannot "cure" a patient. It is the suffering patient who must come to understand his malady ... and by understanding it, banish it.

As we went over John R's history, a picture began to emerge of an interesting and satisfying life. Married, three children. He own business, which probably took up too much of his time, but was doing well. I also heard a familiar litany of suffering and pain—a chronic bad back of mysterious origins, sometimes including such severe pain that he could not get out of bed in the morning. His long and unsuccessful search for relief—experiments with alternative medicine, prescription drugs, and finally, in desperation, surgery—immensely expensive and only temporarily successful. Then the sudden onset of brand-new ailments: sciatica, migraine headaches, acid reflux—the list of maladies went on and on.

As a physician, my heart went out to him. It was my job to help him. But I could only lead. Would John R follow? Would he understand the profound interconnectedness of mind and body? Would he grasp the awesome power of buried rage?

To the uninitiated, there is often something mysterious about mindbody medicine. In truth, the relationship of the mind to the body is no more mysterious than the relationship of the heart to the circulation of the blood, or that of any other organ to the workings of the human body. My first interview with John R indicated he would be open to the idea of mindbody medicine. Within a month of beginning treatment, his pains, which had tortured him for much of his adult life, simply disappeared, without the use of drugs or radical proce-dures. I still get an annual Christmas card from him. In his most recent one he reported that he continues playing tennis and skiing. Last summer he and his oldest boy walked the entire Appalachian Trail. The pain and the equally unexplained other disorders have not returned.

Many of my patients have an initial difficulty grasping the full dynamics of the mindbody syndrome. It is one thing to accept the concept that the mind has great power over the body, but quite another to internalize that knowledge, and to understand it on a deeply personal basis. Even when my patients come to fully appreciate the central element of the equation—that it is their *mind* that contains the root cause of their physical distress—they may continue to stumble over the secondary details, unable to accept the reality of their own buried rage, and remain puzzled over the fact that their own mind can make decisions of which they are unaware.

Sometimes it helps my patients to understand the mindbody connection if they step back and look at it from a broader perspective. Psychosomatic disorders belong to a larger group of entities known as *psychogenic* disorders, which can be defined as any physical disorders induced or modified by the brain for psychological reasons.

Some of these manifestations are commonplace and familiar to all, such as the act of blushing, or the feeling of butterflies in the stomach, or perspiring when in the spotlight. But these are harmless and temporary phenomena, persisting only as long as the unusual stimulus remains.

A second group of psychogenetic disorders includes those cases in which the *pain of a physical disorder is intensified* by anxieties and concerns not directly related to the unusual condition. An example would be someone recently involved in a serious automobile accident whose pain may be significantly worsened by concerns about his or her family, job, and so on, not about the injuries. While mainstream medicine tends to ignore almost all psychogenic manifestations, it generally acknowledges this type, recognizing that symptoms may worsen if the patient is anxious. Doctors may refer to this as *emotional overlay.* In my practice, patients have reported that their pain became much more severe when they were informed of the results of a magnetic resonance imaging (MRI) scan that described an abnormality, such as a herniated disk, particularly if surgery was suggested as a possible treatment.

The third psychogenic group is the exact opposite of the second: it covers cases in which there is a *reduction of physical symptoms* in an existing disorder. In one of the earliest studies of pain, Henry Beecher of Harvard reported that in a group of severely wounded soldiers in World War II, it was found that despite the severity of their injuries they often required little or no analgesic medication because their pain was substantially lessened by their becoming aware that they were still alive, being cared for and removed from the dangers of deprivation, hardship, and sudden death.

By far the most important psychogenic categories are the fourth and fifth groups, *hysterical disorders* and *psychosomatic disorders*. Hysterical disorders are mostly of historical interest, although the psychology of both is identical. My experience has been primarily with psychosomatic disorders.

The symptoms of hysterical disorders are often quite bizarre. The patient may experience a wide variety of highly debilitating maladies, including muscle weakness or paralysis, feeling of numbness or tingling, total absence of sensation, blindness, inability to use their vocal cords, and many others, all *without any physical abnormalities in the body to account for such symptoms.*

It is clear from the nature of hysterical symptoms that their origin is indeed "all in the head," to take a pejorative phrase commonly used to refer to psychosomatic symptoms. The absence of any physical change to the body indicates that ht symptoms are generated by powerful emotions in the brain. Just where in the brain, no one can say for sure. One medical authority, Dr. Antonio R. Damasio, has suggested that these emotion-generating centers are located in the hypothalamus, amygdale, basal forebrain, and brain stem. The patients perceive symptoms as though they were originating in the body when the appropriate brain cells are stimulated. These symptoms often have a very strange and unreal quality about them. One of the nineteenth-century pioneers of psychiatry, Josef Breuer, likened them to hallucinations.

Psychosomatic Disorders

By contrast, in the fifth psychogenetic group, psychosomatic disorders, the brain induces actual physical change in the body. An example of this would be tension myositis syndrome (TMS) a painful disorder that we will examine at greater length. In this condition, the brain orders a reduction of blood flow to a specific part of the body, resulting in mild oxygen deprivation, which causes pain and other symptoms, depending on what tissues have been oxygen deprived.

One of the most intriguing aspects of body hysterical and psychosomatic disorders is that they tend to spread through the population in epidemic fashion, almost as if they were bacteriological in nature, which they are not. Edward Shorter, a medical historian, concluded from his study of the medical literature that the incidence of a psychogenic disorder grows to epidemic proportions when the disorder is in vogue. Strange as it may seem, people with an unconscious psychological need for symptoms tent to develop a disorder that is well known, like back pain, hay fever, or eczema. This is not a conscious decision.

A second cause of such epidemics often results when a psychosomatic disorder is misread by the medical profession and is attributed to a structural abnormality, such as a bone spur, herniated disc, etc.

A 1996 study in Norway suggests there is a third condition that fuels such epidemics: the simple fact that medical treatment may be readily available. A paper published in the journal *Lancet* in 1996 described an epidemic in Norway of what is called "whiplash syndrome." People involved in rear-end collisions, though not seriously injured, were developing pain in the neck and shoulders following the incident. Norwegian doctors were puzzled by the epidemic and decided to investigate. They went to Lithuania, a country with no medical insurance, and on the basis of a controlled study determined that the whiplash syndrome simply did not exist in that country. It turned out that the prevalence of whiplash in Norway had less to do with the severity of rear-end collisions that with the fact that it was in vogue; doctors couldn't explain the epidemic and the ready availability of good medical insurance for treatment!

The most important epidemics of psychosomatic disorders are those associated with pain. As will be discussed below, they have become the ailments du jour for millions of Americans. They are "popular" and most of them have been misdiagnosed as being the result of variety of physical structural abnormalities, hence their spread in epidemic fashion.

What is the genesis of a psychosomatic disorder? As we shall see, the cause is to be found in the unconscious regions of the mind, and as we shall also see, its purpose is to deliberately distract the conscious mind.

The type of symptoms and its location in the body is not important so long as it fulfills its purpose of diverting attention from what is transpiring in the unconscious. On occasion, however, the choice of symptom location may even contribute to the diversion process, something that is common with psychosomatic disorders. For example, a man who experiences the acute onset of pain in his arm while swinging a tennis racket will naturally assume that it was something about the swing that hurt his arm. The reality is that his brain has decided that the time is ripe for a physical diversion and chooses that moment to initiate the pain, because the person will assume that it stems from an injury, not a brain-generated physical condition that cause the pain. How does the brain manage this trick? It simply renders a tendon in the arm slightly oxygen deprived, which results in pain. This is how "tennis elbow" got its name. If that sounds bizarre, diabolical, or self-destructive, you will see later that it is in reality a protective maneuver. My colleagues and I have observed it in thousands of patients.

But in time, such a symptom may lose its power to distract. Then the psyche has another trick up its sleeve. It will find another symptom to take its place, one that is viewed by both patient and doctor as "physical," that is, not psychological in origin. For instance, if a treatment—let's say surgery—neutralizes a particular psychogenic symptom, so that the symptom loses its power to distract, the brain will simply find another target and create another set of symptoms. I have called this the *symptom imperative* and it has enormous public health implications, because psychogenic symptoms are commonly misinterpreted and treated as physical disorders. All of a sudden, the "cured" patient has a brand-new disorder that demands medical attention. More distress. More time lost. More expense. This will be documented as we proceed.

Source: John E. Sarno, *The Divided Mind: The Epidemic of Mindbody Disorders*, pp. 7-13. Copyright © 2007 by HarperCollins Publishers. Reprinted with permission.

Closing Activity

Directions

- Read the second excerpt from the book by Dr. Sarno that appears on the following page.
- Respond to the **prompts** that follow.

1. Select what you think is the most **SIGNIFICANT SENTENCE** in this excerpt from Dr. Sarno.

_____

_____

_____

SIGNIFICANT SENTENCE(S) TOOL	**R** Select the sentence(s) you think is the most important in the reading and tell why you selected it.

2. In this excerpt, Dr. Sarno talks about the following **PROBLEM**:

_____

_____

_____

PROBLEM TOOL	**R** Identify the main problem or issue focused on in the reading. Explain why this is a problem.

3. What **QUESTION** would you really like to ask Dr. Sarno about this excerpt?

_____

_____

_____

QUESTION TOOL	<u>R</u> Pose a thought-provoking question(s) to the author about something that caught your attention in the reading.

4. What is your **POINT OF VIEW** on Dr. Sarno's notion that modern medicine places a tremendous amount of attention on dealing with symptoms instead of causes?

_____

_____

_____

_____

_____

POINT OF VIEW TOOL	<u>R</u> Identify the author's point of view (opinion) on the main problem or issue raised in the reading.

Excerpt from *The Divided Mind: The Epidemic of Mindbody Disorders*

By John E. Sarno, M.D.

Then, too, the findings of neuroscience may be totally irrelevant to some areas of clinical medicine. For example, the fact that a positron-emission tomography (PET) scan can identify the areas of the brain that are activated when a person is manifesting anger is not helpful in determining the source of anger, particularly if unconscious processes are involved. Such findings are extremely interesting but of little use if one is trying to help a patient deal with a behavioral problem. Such help can come only from the laborious process of psychological analysis conducted by someone appropriately trained. When I am working with a patient suffering from pain induced by buried rage, it does no good to know which brain nuclei are involved in the pain process. I must help the patient understand the sources of the rage. Experience has demonstrated that such understanding will usually "cure" him. ...

... The world of the unconscious mind, like the history of life, cannot be studied exclusively by hard science. How can one objectively identify and quantify the personality traits and emotions that reside, so to speak, in the unconscious? The idea that powerful unconscious emotions are responsible for mindbody disorders is based on medical history, knowledge of the psyche, physical examination, logical deduction, and trial-and-error therapeutic experimentation. Success in treatment validates the accuracy of diagnosis if one is assured that there is no placebo effect.

Instead of dealing with this messy reality, contemporary medical science has simply discarded the entire concept of mindbody medicine. It would rather deal with mechanical, measurable, chemical realities, than the abstruse phenomena of psychology. It does not want to know that emotions drive the chemical and physical manifestations they have identified, and it has the dangerous idea that treating the chemistry will correct the disorder. Such treatment may indeed modify the symptoms, but that is not the same thing as curing the disorder.

Homework

Directions

- Consider Future Investigations.

- Now that you have examined a variety of ideas in several discipline areas, think about specific problems that you would like to look into and write about in the future.

APPENDICES

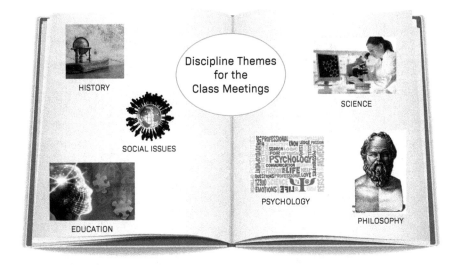

HISTORY

SOCIAL ISSUES

EDUCATION

Discipline Themes
for the
Class Meetings

SCIENCE

PSYCHOLOGY

PHILOSOPHY

The Reading-Writing Thinking Connection: Your Thoughts Your Voice

INVESTIGATION PLAN		
TOPIC TOOL	<u>R</u>	Identify the specific topic that the author has written about.
	<u>W</u>	Select a specific topic to be the focus of your writing.
TITLE TOOL	<u>R</u>	Create a title that expresses the main idea (focus) of the reading.
	<u>W</u>	Create a title that expresses the main idea (focus) of your writing.
PROBLEM TOOL	R	Identify the main problem or issue focused on in the reading. Explain why this is a problem.
	<u>W</u>	Identify the main problem or issue that is the focus of your writing. Explain why this is a problem.
PURPOSE TOOL	<u>R</u>	Explain what you think the author wanted to accomplish through this reading.
	<u>W</u>	Explain what you want to accomplish through your writing.

QUESTION TOOL	**R**	Pose a thought-provoking question(s) to the author about something that caught your attention in the reading.
	W	Pose a thought-provoking question(s) you will investigate and address in your writing.

INVESTIGATION RESEARCH		
INFORMATION /REVIEW OF LITERATURE TOOL	**R**	Identify information and ideas that support and illustrate important points made by the author in the reading.
	W	Search for information and ideas to deepen your understanding and support important points you make in your writing. Cite relevant sources accordingly.
SIGNIFICANT SENTENCE(S) TOOL	**R**	Select the sentence(s) you think is the most important in the reading and tell why you selected it.
	W	Create sentences that express your thoughts and are important to accomplish the purpose of your writing. Elaborate and give examples to make your thoughts clear.
SPEAK IN THE AUTHOR'S VOICE TOOL	**R**	Express ideas, or answer questions, about the reading as if you were the author or an individual in the reading.
	W	Include quotes (or paraphrases of quotes) from selected authors or sources to support and clarify what you want to express in your writing. Cite relevant sources accordingly.
PARAPHRASE TOOL	**R**	Put a sentence(s) from the reading into your own words that capture exactly what the author communicates.
	W	Paraphrase a sentence(s) from what you read to use in your writing.

POINT OF VIEW TOOL	**R**	Identify the author's point of view (opinion) on the main problem or issue raised in the reading.
	W	State your point of view (opinion) on the main problem or issue raised in your writing.
ASSUMPTION TOOL	**R**	Identify what you think the author takes for granted (i.e., accepts as true without proof) in the reading.
	W	State what you take for granted (i.e., accept as true without proof) in your writing.

INVESTIGATION FINDINGS		
CONCLUSION TOOL	**R**	Identify what you think is the most important conclusion that the author came to in the reading and how that conclusion was reached.
	W	State the most important conclusion that you come to in your writing and explain how you reached that conclusion.
RECOMMENDATION TOOL	**R**	State what you think should be done to deal effectively with the main problem or issue addressed in the reading.
	W	State what you think should be done to deal effectively with the main problem or issue you address in your writing.
CONSEQUENCE TOOL	**R**	State what you think could happen if we follow or do not follow what the author or someone in the reading recommends or implies that we do.
	W	State what you think could happen if we follow or do not follow what you recommend or imply in your writing.

SUPPORT TOOLS		
D O X I TOOL	**R**	For a word (concept) in the reading which you think you need to understand better: look up the **D**efinition, put it into your **O**wn words (i.e., paraphrase it), give an e**X**ample of it, and **I**llustrate it.
	W	For a word (concept) you want to use in your writing which you think you need to understand better: look up the **D**efinition, put it into our **O**wn words (i.e., paraphrase it), give an e**X**ample of it, and **I**llustrate it.
GRAMMAR TOOL	**R**	Notice how the author selects and arranges words in their sentences to express what they want to say (i.e., parts of speech, tenses, punctuation).
	W	Select and arrange words in your sentences to express clearly what you want to say (i.e., parts of speech, tenses, punctuation).

	12 STRATEGIES for TEACHING and LEARNING
1	**Discussion-Oriented Student Seating Strategy** Arrange your students' seating in such a way that the students can comfortably see, hear, and communicate with each other across the classroom.
2	**Name Tents and Randomly Assigned Seating Strategy** Use a "name tent" for each of your students so that you can call them by their names from the first time you see them and seat them randomly every class session.
3	**Use of a Speaker's Voice Strategy** Explain to your students that each time they speak, they should use a strong, clear voice that can be heard by everyone in the classroom.
4	**Popcorn Read Strategy** Let students know that when you say "popcorn read," it means "someone" should read—in a loud, clear voice—the part(s) of the lesson that you have indicated (e.g., a direction, sentence, reading excerpt).
5	**Clear and Complete Sentences (Written and Spoken Thoughts) Strategy** Direct your students to respond to Prompts and extended writing activities using clear and complete sentences (thoughts).
6	**Circulate-to-Guide Strategy** Move around the room to offer suggestions, pointers, and guidance to your students as they work on the lessons in the classroom.

7	**Timed-Activities with Clear, Concise, Written Directions Strategy** Communicate to your students that for every activity there are written directions to follow and a specific amount of time is given in which that activity should be completed.
8	**Zenergy Chime Signal Strategy** Signal your class using a Zenergy Chime to capture their attention when a new phase of an activity is about to begin.
9	**"Call On Students" Strategy** Call on students to share their responses to prompts and to questions you pose spontaneously, rather than asking for volunteers or allowing students to call out answers.
10	**"I Don't Know Yet" Strategy** Tell your students that when you call on them and they don't know the answer, to please pause to reflect and answer, "I don't know yet."
11	**Collaborative Activities Strategy** Cultivate thoughtful discussion by having groups of two or more students work together to discuss and evaluate thoughts that they have written independently, prior to getting together.
12	**Stand Up and Move Strategy** Have your students get out of their seats to move somewhere in the classroom to discuss their responses to prompts.

Use of the 12 Strategies for Teaching and Learning, as explained in this section, is essential to effectively carrying out the lessons contained in this book (see the previous page for a chart with a brief description of each of the 12 Strategies for Teaching and Learning). Below is explained **how** each Strategy works, and the **purpose** of each Strategy. Also, an **example** of each Strategy's use is given. Using these Strategies along with the specially-designed Tools of OUR THINKING TOOLBOX will help you establish a "Culture of Thinking" in your classroom.

1. Discussion-Oriented Student Seating Strategy

How it works

In the "Discussion-Oriented Student Seating Strategy," you arrange your students' seating in such a way that the students can comfortably see, hear, and communicate with each other across the classroom. This is naturally accomplished by arranging individual chairs in a semicircle; or, where students are seated at tables, by arranging the tables in a horseshoe or "U" shape (often referred to as a "seminar" configuration). Either of these classroom seating arrangements works effectively with classes of up to thirty-five students.

Most classrooms are set up in a series of rows—typically six across and five or six deep. For two reasons, this arrangement does not lead to high-quality learning. First, in this "lecture" configuration, students have been programmed to sit passively while information is given to them from the front of the room. Second, student-to-student discussion, i.e., exchange of ideas and points of view, is minimized when students see only the backs of the heads in front of them. Research and experience tell us that the involvement of all students in the active exchange of ideas and perspectives is a basic necessity in the creation of a community of learners. Discussion-Oriented Student Seating predisposes your classroom to this exchange and this creation of community. Once your students realize through experience the benefits of this classroom arrangement, they will gladly help you set up the room for the lesson and, when the lesson is over, return the seats to the "usual" pattern of rows. You will find that with several students assisting this way, it takes less than two minutes to rearrange the room.

Its purpose

The purpose of the "Discussion-Oriented Student Seating Strategy" is to make it possible for your students to discuss their thoughts and points of view with each other. This discussion builds their communication skills. As students repeatedly respond to prompts with independent thoughts about what they are reading and engage in "peer discussions" of one another's investigative articles, you will find that a subtle change takes place. For one, students become more sincerely interested in hearing what their classmates have to say. This is because the responses and writing shared are the creative products of human minds, not mechanical answers lifted directly out of the reading. Students naturally take interest in sharing such thinking. Colorful and eloquent, but only marginally relevant comments and writing are minimized because the students' thoughts have resulted from using the "thinking-centered" Tools of OUR THINKING TOOLBOX. Focused, substantial thinking is the order of the day. Discussion-Oriented Student Seating creates an environment for this interchange of ideas to take place.

Example

An example of the "Discussion-Oriented Student Seating Strategy" is the following:

It is the first day of the class. You are standing in front of the classroom as students enter. Without your having to say a word, they notice two things: (1) the seating arrangement is such that all can see each other and hiding is not possible; and (2) with "Name Tents" out (see Strategy #2 below), it is clear where students are to sit. From this point on, as you conduct *each class meeting* using all the 12 Strategies, this "Discussion-Oriented Student Seating Strategy" will naturally invite student learning. You will often hear from your students such comments as: "I wish my other classes were set up and run like this," or "Because the way the seating is arranged, I feel we are able to communicate with each other much better."

2. Name Tents and Randomly Assigned Seating Strategy

How it works

The "Name Tents and Randomly Assigned Seating Strategy" has two parts: (1) the use of a "Name Tent" for each of your students from the first to the last class meeting; and (2) "Randomly Assigned Seating" of all your students for every class session. Name Tents can readily be made using five-by-eight-inch index cards, folded in half the long way, on which you write each student's first name (see graphic representation below after "Example").

These Name Tents should be created from your class roster before the first class meeting. Experience shows that bringing at least five to ten blank Name Tents is often useful, so students who are "crashing" the class can write their names on the blank Name Tents and be easily and immediately added to joint activities. This strategy complements the "Call On Students Strategy" (see Strategy #9 below) and the "Discussion-Oriented Student Seating Strategy." The use of these three strategies in combination creates a classroom environment that promotes both independent thinking and the interchange of ideas—two benefits of inestimable value.

Its purpose

The "Name Tents and Randomly Assigned Seating Strategy" accomplishes six purposes. First, by placing Name Tents on students' seats or desks, you will be able to call on each student by her or his name from the very first time you see that student to the last class of the semester. Our own names have a special meaning to and significance for us. Having students see a seat with their name already on it, identifying a place meant for them, and calling on them using their names without hesitation communicates to them that they are already recognized and appreciated by the teacher. This allows you to immediately make that special, significant connection with each student. Second, Name Tents, especially when used with the "Discussion-Oriented Student Seating Strategy," allow students to call each other by name. This helps to create a better functioning classroom community. Third, Name Tents greatly help you in your use of the Call On Students Strategy. Fourth, taking attendance can be done in a matter of moments, without using valuable class time, by noting in your records which students are not sitting behind their Name Tents. Fifth, when your students find that their Name Tents are placed on classroom seats in random order (i.e., Randomly Assigned Seating) at every class session, they recognize that they are being invited and expected to fully participate and learn. They quickly understand that they will not be able to hide or sit only with friends. Sixth, since the lessons in this book make regular use of the "Collaborative Activities Strategy (see Strategy #11 below)," Randomly Assigned Seating for every class meeting provides students with the benefit of working with different classmates throughout the course, a most valuable experience for their personal, intellectual, and social growth.

Example

An example of the "Name Tents and Randomly Assigned Seating Strategy" is the following:
   It is the first class meeting of the course. Your students, on entering the classroom, notice your semicircular arrangement of seats (or desks/tables) and see that Name Tents have been placed on each seat (or are spread out on each desk or table). Abigail will naturally sit where she sees a Name Tent that has "**ABIGAIL**" printed on it, as the rest of the class members

similarly will sit by their own Name Tents. Your students immediately have an experience of Randomly Assigned Seating in an overall discussion-oriented design simply by entering your classroom for the first time. The purpose and value of being in such a classroom environment soon becomes clear to them. In fact, they often wonder aloud why their other classes are not arranged this way. At the end of this first class meeting, you ask your students to drop their Name Tents in a little box on the way out. As students arrive for the next class meeting (and all successive meetings), they see that the Name Tents have once again been placed on the arms of seats (or on desks/tables)—this time, randomly *different* seats.

Guiding Note

1. It is critical to begin the semester with the Name Tents visible, as part of instructional procedure, so the notion will take firm root in the students' minds.
2. At the end of each class, storage of Name Tents is easy, since you can collect all the Name Tents, collapse them, and put a rubber band around the whole class set.

3. Use of a Speaker's Voice Strategy

How it works

Introduce the "Use of a Speaker's Voice Strategy" at the earliest appropriate opportunity during the first class meeting. Explain to your students that each time they speak, they should use a strong, clear voice that can be heard by everyone in the classroom. Then call on a few students to read a sentence or two they wrote in response to a particular prompt. Often a student does not realize that people have trouble hearing her or him. From the very first class to the very last class meeting, the students should be constantly reminded that the "Use of a Speaker's Voice" is always required. In other words, students must know that it is never acceptable to speak to the class in a voice that is not audible to everyone.

Its purpose

The purpose of the "Use of a Speaker's Voice Strategy" is to help students recognize and remember that you and their classmates consider their ideas to be important and want to hear them – their "voices" need to be heard. They do, indeed, have something to say, so their ideas and voices certainly should be heard. Because students develop and share their own thoughts about what they read and write in every lesson, it is natural that they want to hear each other and want to be heard. Such sharing of ideas can be achieved only when students regularly use a "Speaker's Voice."

Example

An example of the "Use of a Speaker's Voice Strategy" is the following:

During an Opening Activity as your students work on their INVESTIGATION PLANS, they are asked to respond the prompt, "Review the **QUESTION** Tool (the "W" version) below to create two key QUESTIONS you will use to focus your investigation." After circulating around the room to see how the students are doing, you sound the Zenergy Chime (see Strategy #8 below) and call on Maria to read her response to the prompt. Maria does respond, but in a soft voice. You say: "Maria, remember to speak so Yvette"—a student seated amongst those furthest from Maria—"can hear you. She came all the way to this class to hear what you have to say." Saying something like this lightens the feeling in the classroom and still sends a clear, appropriate message to Maria to make sure "your voice is heard." In this situation, you also could have said, "Maria, you have posed two good questions. Let's make sure everyone gets to hear it." If students do not practice this in your class, under your caring guidance, where else will they get this chance to gain confidence in "voice"?

4. Popcorn Read Strategy

How it works

On the first day of class, explain to your students that from the very first activity of the first class meeting through all of the 30 class meetings they will be asked to "Popcorn Read," which you will explain "right now." Tell them that this simply means *"someone"* should read— in a loud, clear voice, so that everyone can hear her or him—the part(s) of the lesson that you have indicated, e.g., a direction, a sentence, a prompt, a paragraph, or a reading excerpt, etc. Finally, explain that, rather than raising their hands to "Popcorn Read," someone should voluntarily and randomly begin to read aloud.

Its purpose

The purpose of the "Popcorn Reading Strategy" is to place the initiative in the students' hands and to encourage their active involvement in the class. Also, in this way, students will become used to hearing, and expecting to hear, their own and others' voices, rather than falling into the habit of passively expecting that you will do most of the talking.

Example

An example of the "Popcorn Read Strategy" is the following:

As you begin an activity on the first day, you give students the following instruction: "'Popcorn Read' the quote you see here": [*The aim of education should be to teach students how to think rather than what to think*" (John Dewey)]. One student self-selects to "Popcorn Read" the quote, reading it out to the rest of the class in a strong, clear "Speaker's Voice."

5. Clear and Complete Sentences (Written and Spoken Thoughts) Strategy

How it works

Throughout this book, students are directed to use clear and complete sentences (thoughts) as they respond to prompts and for the investigative articles they write. In this way, students constantly practice creating and communicating complete sentences (written and spoken thoughts) as they work through both in-class work and homework. One-word responses, truncated as well as rambling thoughts, and "texting" language are not acceptable here. Responding in such unclear phrases prevents the development of depth and complexity in thinking. Students' minds have to capture and articulate their thoughts on what they have read as they respond to prompts, and as they write extensively. In so doing, they learn how to interact with a text in a holistic and most profound way and to write articles that contribute to the body of knowledge on important problems.

Its purpose

The constant practice of creating complete sentences (thoughts) that is required throughout this book disciplines students' minds and refines their thinking. Further, it develops their capacity to think deeply and to communicate clearly.

Example

An example of the "Clear and Complete Sentences (Written and Spoken Thoughts) Strategy" is the following:

   Before your students begin to read and respond to five prompts concerning a book excerpt by Dr. John E. Sarno on mindbody disorders, direct them to: "Make sure you write complete sentences as you respond to the prompts." Subsequently, as you circulate around the room checking students' written responses, you guide those who have not responded in a complete sentence to do so. In this way, as the students work, you are reinforcing the emphasis of the initial instructions to think and write only in clear and complete sentences (thoughts). You provide the same guidance as they write each part of their investigative articles.

6. Circulate-to-Guide Strategy

How it works

In the "Circulate-to-Guide Strategy," you move around the room to offer suggestions, pointers, and guidance to the students as they work on the lessons in the classroom. As you apply this strategy, you are in effect the "Reading and Writing Coach." Your students are your "Reading and Writing Team." Your goal is to bring them to a high level of skill in the art of reading and in the art of the written word. A useful way to help them accomplish this goal is to "coach" them while they are in the act of writing based on their thoughts about what they have read or the for the extensive writing of their Investigative Articles. Since every activity in this book requires students to think about what they read and what they write, you continually have this opportunity to coach them to become more and more skilled readers and writers. Use of "Discussion-Oriented Student Seating," presented above, effectively maximizes the benefits of the "Circulate to-Guide Strategy," since it helps you to reach and coach your students in a timely and effective way.

Its purpose

The purpose of using the "Circulate-to-Guide Strategy" is to provide immediate feedback while your students are actually writing as they think either about what they are reading or drafting their Investigative Articles. This allows you to see where individual students', as well as the class's, strengths and needs are, and thus, to provide guidance and encouragement accordingly. By directly seeing what your students understand and are able to do, you can help them, in a timely way, to become aware of the adjustments they need to make. Also, you can make timely, appropriate instructional adjustments to address their needs. Using this strategy, you are constantly observing and addressing "teachable moments". As you circulate around the classroom to guide the students as they work, they come to realize that they must put their full attention into their reading, writing, and thinking in order to benefit from your guidance and support. They also will come to expect and value your guidance and support.

Example

An example of the "Circulate-to-Guide Strategy" is the following:

Your class has begun work on Part 2 of their Investigative Article, INVESTIGATION RESEARCH and in the Main Activity students are asked to respond to the following prompt: "How would you respond if a friend asks you, 'What are two things I should do to take good notes from the sources I find for my investigation?'" You begin walking around the classroom. Once you see that several students have begun to write their responses to the prompt, you begin to comment to individual students on their responses. For example, as you see Ramon has written "important information" in response to the prompt, you direct a question and an idea to him: "I like your thinking here, but is this a complete sentence? Elaborate on this thought to give your friend a more complete idea how best to proceed." As you circulate to guide your students, "teachable moments like this," will present themselves time and again.

7. Timed-Activities with Clear, Concise Written Directions Strategy

How it works

It is important to communicate to your students that for every activity a specific amount of time is given in which that activity should be completed. Again, this can be adjusted as needed, but the students should know clearly, at the beginning of each activity, the amount of time in which they must complete the activity. Further, by providing clear, concise written directions, your students will understand exactly what it is they are to do within the time allotted.

Its purpose

The purpose of the "Timed-Activities with Clear, Concise Written Directions Strategy" is to help students learn to focus and keep their attention on the activity they are doing. Planning definite amounts of time along with clear, concise written directions for each activity gives you, at the same time, a definite plan for how to pace each lesson. You thus have a solid starting point from which to modify the pacing and directions for your students. As you help students maintain this kind of focus, you will find that it is not necessary to ask students "Are you done yet?"

Example

An example of the "Timed-Activities with Clear, Concise Written Directions Strategy" is the following:

You have your students work on the Closing Activity of Class #9 in this book and ask someone to "Popcorn Reads" the DIRECTIONS. You then let them know that they have 40 minutes to work on this activity in the LAB.

8. Zenergy Chime Signal Strategy

How it works

In the "Zenergy Chime Signal Strategy," the teacher signals the class using a Zenergy Chime (see image below). This chime produces a pleasant yet penetrating tone that cuts through the sounds of even dozens of people engaged in discussion.

Its purpose

The purpose of the "Zenergy Chime Signal Strategy" is to capture your students' attention when the next phase of an activity is about to begin or when you want their attention for a moment. It provides an effective, nonverbal way to indicate that you would like everyone to stop what they are doing. Yelling over the students to get their attention is no longer necessary, which creates a more peaceful classroom environment. When you use this strategy, students hear your voice associated only with words of guidance and support, with leading discussions, and with providing directions for activities.

Example

An example of the "Zenergy Chime Signal Strategy" is the following:

Your students are carrying out a "Peer Discussion" activity. You circulate among them to guide them in their work. You had told them at the beginning of this activity that it should take fifteen minutes. Seeing that after fifteen minutes many could benefit by taking five more minutes to finish their discussions, you sound the Zenergy Chime once, followed by an orchestra conductor's "cutoff" motion (i.e., using both arms coming to a complete stop right in front of you). The students stop what they are doing and give you their attention. You let them know to take five more minutes to finish their discussions so everyone will be ready to bring things together in the next phase of this activity—whole-class sharing.

9. Call On Students Strategy

How it works

In all lesson activities, call on as the main way you have students share their responses to prompts, and to questions that you pose spontaneously to your class. Use of "Name Tents" as described above, makes this possible. You should use the "Call On Students Strategy" rather than asking for volunteers or allowing students to call out answers.

Its purpose

The purpose of using the "Call On Students Strategy" is to maximize students' involvement and attention in class. Once students see that you will be calling on them as the principal means of sharing, their attention level will increase dramatically. When this strategy is used, students understand that they must take all activities seriously and apply their minds to what they and their classmates are reading, writing, hearing, and saying. Most importantly, this strategy helps students gain confidence in their ability to express their thoughts in front of others. They come to the realization that they can think for themselves, and share those thoughts, when given the opportunity.

Example

An example of the "Call on Students Strategy" is the following:

Your class has just read a speech by Cesar Chavez, and the students have responded to four prompts. You sound the Zenergy Chime to tell your students it is time to share some of the thoughts they have come to. "Naomi, share your response to the prompt: 'What do you think was the main PROBLEM Cesar Chavez raised in his speech?'" After Naomi reads what she has written, you respond to her thought, provide your feedback, and call on a few more students similarly. Follow this with a brief discussion of the ideas that were shared.

Guiding Note

1. You may think that calling on students, or on some particular students, "puts them on the spot." The opposite is true. Students come to your class to learn to read and write well. By allowing them to not participate, you are putting them and their future "on the spot." Many students will choose not to participate and leave it to others to share their thoughts and answer your questions. When students habitually choose to "hide" or to passively evade participation year after year, this creates a sense of learned helplessness in them. This sense of helplessness leads to mental inactivity and a loss of opportunities to gain confidence in having their voices heard. Under your caring guidance, the "Call On Students Strategy" will create a new sense of self-confidence in your students through the intellectual engagement which answering your questions and sharing their own thoughts with the class naturally brings about.

2. Teachers pose many questions during a given lesson to accomplish two main goals: (1) to get students to think about what has been asked, and (2) to get a good sense of how well students understand the information, concepts, and ideas involved. When you use the "Call On Students Strategy" the possibility of accomplishing both of these

goals is greatly increased. When students realize that calling out or volunteering to respond to questions posed are going to be the norm, it becomes it becomes extremely difficult to accomplish either goal.

10. "I Don't Know Yet" Strategy

How it works

The "I Don't Know Yet Strategy" is an important aid in fostering in your students a healthy outlook on learning. At some point early during the first class meeting, a student on whom you have called to share her or his response will likely say, "I don't know." At this moment, say to the class, with a most positive and supportive feeling, "When I call on you for a response, I want everyone to feel free to say, 'I don't know.' I want also, however, that when you say 'I don't know,' add one word—'yet.' From now on, when you don't know the answer, please pause to reflect and answer, 'I don't know yet.' We are here to learn. Of course, there are things that we don't know yet. That is why we are here to work together. We will certainly come to know the answers and gain understanding as time goes on!"

Its purpose

The purpose of the "I Don't Know Yet Strategy" is that it fundamentally changes students' perceptions of themselves as learners. As you and your students use this book and the 12 Strategies for Teaching and Learning, you will find that the appropriate environment is naturally created in which students will say, "I don't know yet," and mean it! Usually, when students have said in class, "I don't know," it almost always meant, "I don't know, nor do I care to know"; or, "I don't know, and I am not capable of knowing"; or, "I don't know, and I didn't even hear what you asked me." By saying, "I don't know yet," and meaning it, students gain a new confidence in their learning abilities. Students come to realize that *every answer given sincerely is a step in learning toward greater understanding*. The message here is a critical one for all of their future endeavors, both in school and in life.

Example

An example of the "I Don't Know Yet Strategy" is the following:

On the first day of class, you have just asked your students to paraphrase, in a clear and complete sentence, the following Ethiopian Proverb:

"Until lions have their own historians, the hunter will always be glorified."

After everyone has worked independently to paraphrase this proverb, you call on several students to read what they have written. When you call on Andy, he says, "I don't know."

You immediately go to the whiteboard and write, "I don't know." You then tell the students that for the rest of the semester, add one word to their answer whenever they say, "I don't know." You then say and write "yet'" after what you just wrote. You tell the students, "Working together using **OUR THINKING TOOLBOX** to become artists of reading and the written word, we will 'know.' Each answer you give will help you and your classmates move one step more toward understanding and knowing."

Guiding Note

It is worth noting out here that as you introduce this Strategy you can point out to your students the following:

> "Thomas Edison, when asked how it felt to be the person who created the light bulb, responded by saying, 'You are looking at the man who created 9,999 light bulbs that did not work.'"

The message the students realize as they think about Edison's words reinforces the full meaning and value of saying, "I don't know yet."

11. Collaborative Activities Strategy

How it works

In this book, the Collaborative Activities are those that involve two or more students working together to discuss and evaluate thoughts which they have written independently prior to getting together. The three types of Collaborative Activities are: (1) Pair Share, (2) Jigsaw (Home and Expert Groups), and (3) Peer Discussion.

Its purpose

The purpose of the "Collaborative Activities Strategy" is to cultivate thoughtful discussion of the wealth of ideas which are created by students in every lesson. This strategy encourages and supports the students to discuss their thoughts and perspectives with each other. It allows their voices to be heard, and they realize they have minds that can think purposefully about purposeful things. Where else will they have the opportunity to do this during every activity of every lesson at school but in your class as you use this book with **OUR THINKING TOOLBOX**? This is their chance, under your caring and skilled guidance.

An example of the "Collaborative Activities Strategy" used in a learning activity is the following:

Your students are asked to, "Have a 'Peer Discussion' with your partner to give recommendations for your partner's draft (Word document) of the **"Solutions"** and the **"Roadblocks"** subsections of the INVESTIGATION RESEARCH. Then, they are asked to, "Discuss your recommendations with your partner."

12. Stand Up and Move Strategy

How it works

The "Stand Up and Move Strategy" involves having your students get out of their seats to move somewhere in the classroom in order to discuss their responses to prompts. You can have them move anywhere from a few feet to clear across the classroom to engage in these discussions.

Its purpose

The purpose of the "Stand Up and Move Strategy" is to give the students a periodic physical break during the lesson through purposeful movement. While the many different prompts, writing assignments, and types of readings provide rich variety for intellectual stimulation, that effect is enhanced by coupling it periodically with kinesthetic stimulation. Moving physically after mental work provides a sense of relief and refreshes students. While the Jigsaw type of Collaborative Activity lends itself particularly well to having students move around in the classroom, using your judgment, you can also employ the "Stand Up and Move Strategy" for "Peer Discussions," work in the Lab, or at any other time that seems beneficial.

Example

An example of the "Stand Up and Move Strategy" is the following:

Your students are completing the first phase of a "Main Activity," which you began by having them get into "Home Groups" of three and identifying who the "A," "B," and "C" persons were, respectively (with each person in the "Home Group" working on a different, yet related, aspect of this particular assignment). While circulating around the room, you see that everyone has completed her or his independent work. By sounding the Zenergy Chime, you indicate that the next phase of the activity, which involves "Expert Groups," is going to begin. You tell the class that the "A's" will now go and stand in one part of the room to discuss their responses, while the "B's" and the "C's" will discuss their responses in two other parts of the classroom. Once the "A's," "B's," and "C's" get to their respective locations, you spend "coaching time" with each group as they discuss their thoughts. You then ask everyone to go back to their "Home Groups" to share their own ideas, as well as the ideas from their respective "Expert Groups" concerning the different aspects of the assignment they worked on.

Source Notes

For: _____

Bibliographic Information	Date Notes Taken: _____

Author(s): _____

Name of Book, Article, Website, (& URL):

_____

Page(s): _____

Publication Date: _____ City, State: _____

Publisher: _____

Pg(s)	Para(s)	Line(s)	Notes (Direct Quotes or Paraphrases)/ My Comments and Ideas

BIBLIOGRAPHY OF READINGS

Bowman, Chris. 2007. "Company Took Lead Warning Off Free Lunchboxes: State-Issued Bags Promoted Health." San Diego Union-Tribune. http://www.signonsandiego.com/uniontrib/20070927/news_1n27lunchbox.html

Carson, Rachel. 1962. *Silent Spring*. Houghton Mifflin, Boston, MA. http://core.ecu.edu/soci/juskaa/SOCI3222/carson.html

Chávez, César. 1991. "Statement from César Chávez." In *The Words of Cesar Chavez*, edited by Richard Jensen and John Hammerback.

Cousins, N. 1979. *Anatomy of an Illness as Perceived by the Patient*. New York: W. W. Norton & Company. http://books.google.com/books/about/Anatomy_of_an_illness_as_perceived_by_th.html?id=zzavpKwYsDEC

Einstein, Albert. 1950. *Out of My Later Years*. Kensington Publishing Corp. New York, NY.

Haworth, Alan. 2004. "Socrates (the Philosopher)." In *Understanding the Political Philosophers: From Ancient to Modern Times*, 8–9. Taylor & Francis Group. Oxfordshire, UK.

King, Martin Luther. 1963. "Letter from Birmingham Jail." http://www.africa.upenn.edu/Articles_Gen/Letter_Birmingham.html

Lockwood, Alan H. 2012. *The Silent Epidemic: Coal and the Hidden Threat to Health*. Cambridge, MA: MIT Press.

Malcolm X. (1964). The Autobiography of Malcolm X: As told to Alex Haley. Ballantine Publishing Group, a division of Random House Inc. New York, NY.

Parade Magazine. 2007. "The Worry Over Lead in Lipsticks." December 2007, 19.

Ramananda, Swami. (1965). *Evolutionary Outlook on Life*. Kankhal, India: Sadhana Parivar.

San Diego Union-Tribune. 2007. "Public School Students Flunk Physical Fitness." December 9, 2007. http://www.signonsandiego.com/uniontrib/20071209/news_lz1m9theweek.html

Sarno, John E. 2007. *The Divided Mind: The Epidemic of Mindbody Disorders*, HarperCollins Publishers, New York, NY.

Washington, Booker T. (1911). *My Larger Education*. Doubleday, Page & Company, Garden City, New York. http://www.btwsociety.org/library/books/My_Larger_Education/06.php

Wintz, Cary D. 1995. *African American Political Thought*, 1890–1930: Washington, Du Bois, Garvey, and Randolph. Routledge, UK.

Zinn, Howard. 2005. "Columbus, the Indians, and Human Progress." In *A People's History of the United States*, 1–3. Ward & Balkin Agency, Inc. Lowell, MA http://www.historyisaweapon.com/defcon1/zinncol1.html

ABOUT THE AUTHORS

Suzanne Borman

- Formerly professor at the Hufstedler School of Education, Alliant International University, San Diego, California

- Doctorate in education, Teachers College, Columbia University

- Formerly special day teacher, the Mountain Empire Unified School District; elementary teacher at Tenth Street School ("Port-of-Entry School"), Los Angeles Unified School District; and special education teacher, the New York City School System

- Presenter at National Association for Developmental Education (NADE), and College Reading and Learning Association (CRLA) Annual Conferences and the International Conference on Critical Thinking, held annually in Berkeley, California

- Coauthor with William Borman, Sylvia Garcia-Navarrete, Joel Levine, and Yuki Yamamoto of *OUR READING TOOLBOX, First Edition* (2016); coauthor with Joel Levine of *Critical Thinking for Children: Teachers' Manual II, Foundation for Critical Thinking* (2010); coauthor with Joel Levine of *A Practical Guide to Elementary Instruction: From Plan to Delivery* (1997)

William Borman

- Formerly assistant and adjunct professor of philosophy at various schools, including, visiting scholar at UCLA, assistant professor/visiting scholar Columbia University; adjunct at New York Institute of Technology; visiting scholar and research associate, at Humboldt University, Berlin; adjunct professor/visiting scholar at Ludwig Maximillians Universitaet, Munich; adjunct at Chapman University, San Diego, California; adjunct, Grossmont Community College, El Cajon, California; adjunct, LaGuardia Community College (CUNY)

- Doctorate in philosophy, City University of New York

- Formerly philosophical counselor, private practice, San Diego, California

- Formerly executive producer and host of *Gandhi in the Park*, WBAI-FM, New York City

- Numerous presentations, nationally and internationally, on Gandhi, peace studies, Socrates, Wittgenstein, and ethics

- Coauthor with Suzanne Borman, Sylvia Garcia-Navarrete, Joel Levine, and Yuki Yamamoto, of *OUR READING TOOLBOX, First Edition* (2016); author of *Gandhi and Non-violence* (1989); *The Other Side of Death: Upanishadic Eschatology* (1990); *Thanatology and Philosophy: Death, Eschatology, and Immortality* (1993)

Sylvia Garcia-Navarrete

- Professor of English, reading, and English as a second language (ESL), Southwestern College, Chula Vista, California

- Adjunct faculty (EdD, MA, and BA programs), Administration, Rehabilitation and Postsecondary Education, (ARPE), San Diego State University

- Doctorate in educational leadership, San Diego State University (SDSU), in community college/postsecondary education leadership, San Diego, California; secretary/treasurer, SDSU Community College Leadership Alumni Chapter, of SDSU Alumni Association

- Master's degree in education, with an emphasis on reading, National University, San Diego, California

- ACCJC Pilot Accreditation Standard II, faculty lead

- Committee member at Southwestern College: Student Equity and Achievement Program Committee; Student Learning Outcomes (SLO), committee member; and liaison between SLO and the reading/ESL department faculty; Faculty lead, Organizational Leadership Academy

- Co-chair, Student Equity Planning Subcommittee

- Workshop presenter at annual conferences of NADE, California Association for Developmental Education (CalADE), League for Innovation, CRLA, National Institute for Staff and Organizational Development (NISOD), and the International Conference on Critical Thinking, held annually in Berkeley, California, as well as at numerous colleges and school sites, internationally, nationally, and throughout California

- International presenter at Instituto Michoacano de Ciencias de la Educacion (IMCED) in Morelia, Michoacán, MX

- Past president of CalADE, California Chapter of NADE, 2012–2013

- Coauthor with Suzanne Borman, William Borman, Joel Levine, and Yuki Yamamoto of *OUR READING TOOLBOX, First Edition* (2016)

- Publication: NADE Digest, Fall, 2012; coauthored with Joel Levine and Caren Sax *Our Reading Toolbox: The Reading-Thinking Connection in a Community College Developmental Reading Class*

- Awards and recognitions: "Certificate of Recognition for Outstanding Service to Our Community in the Field of Education" from California State Assembly woman, Dr. Shirley Weber 79th District; "Outstanding Latino/a Faculty in Higher Education for Service/Teaching in Higher Education (Teaching Institutions)" Award, from American Association of Hispanics in Higher Education, San Antonio, Texas, 2013; "Teaching Excellence" Award, from NISOD, Austin, Texas, 2011 and 2012; Academic Senate Faculty Award, Southwestern College, Chula Vista, California, 2012; Adjunct Faculty Award, Southwestern College, Chula Vista, California, 2011; Scholarship Recipient, NADE, Washington, DC, 2011

Joel Levine

- Dean of School of Language, Literature, and Humanities at Southwestern College, Chula Vista, California

- Doctorate in education, Teachers College, Columbia University

- Formerly director of the Center for Critical Thinking; director of teacher education at Alliant International University (formerly United States International University), San Diego, California; and director of teacher education at Mount St. Mary's College, Los Angeles, California

- Formerly, classroom teacher, Los Angeles Unified School District and New York City School System

- Workshop presenter at NADE, CalADE, CRLA, NISOD, the International Conference on Critical Thinking, held annually in Berkeley, California, as well as at numerous colleges and schools around the country

- Coauthor with Suzanne Borman, William Borman, Sylvia Garcia-Navarrete, and Yuki Yamamoto of *OUR READING TOOLBOX, First Edition* (2016); coauthor with Suzanne Borman of *Critical Thinking For Children: Teachers' Manual II, Foundation for Critical Thinking* (2010); coauthor with Suzanne Borman of *A Practical Guide to Elementary Instruction: From Plan to Delivery* (1997); author of *Secondary Instruction: A Manual for Classroom Teaching* (1989)

Yuki Yamamoto

- Professor of ESL/Japanese as a foreign language (JFL), at the community college and university levels, and in various vocational settings; ESL Placement Assessment Committee, chair; Learning English for Academic Purposes, program level co-lead at Southwestern College, Chula Vista, California; and SLO level lead, Cuyamaca College, El Cajon, California

- Master's degree in Teaching English to speakers of other languages (TESOL), education, from United States International University/Alliant International University in San Diego, California; BA in philosophy, Waseda University, Tokyo, Japan

- TESOL certificate teacher trainer, University of California, San Diego, California

- Past president of CalADE, California Chapter of NADE, 2014–2015

- Workshop presenter at California Teachers of English to Speakers of Other Languages (CATESOL) regional- and state-level conferences and at numerous national and state professional conferences, including NADE, CRLA, NISOD, CalADE, and the International Conference on Critical Thinking held annually in Berkeley, California

- Faculty award winner at several institutions: "Adjunct Faculty Award" from Southwestern College, 2009; "Excellence Award" from NISOD, 2009; and nominated for "Adjunct Faculty Award," Cuyamaca College, El Cajon, California, 2008

- Coauthor with Suzanne Borman, William Borman, Sylvia Garcia-Navarrete, and Joel Levine of *OUR READING TOOLBOX, First Edition* (2016)

CPSIA information can be obtained
at www.ICGtesting.com
Printed in the USA
LVHW051044290721
693959LV00008B/43

9 781516 537877